Anna Åberg
Mogens Rüdiger

Energy
in the Nordic World

Aarhus University Press / The University of Wisconsin Press

The Nordic World
Energy in the Nordic World
© Anna Åberg og Mogens Rüdiger 2024

Cover, layout, and typesetting:
Camilla Jørgensen, Trefold
Cover photograph: Ulrika Ernström
Copy editors: Heidi Flegal and Mia Gaudern
Acquisitions editors: Amber Rose Cederström
and Karina Bell Ottosen
This book is typeset in FS Ostro and printed
on Munken Lynx 130 g
Printed by Narayana Press, Denmark
Printed in Denmark 2024

ISBN 978 87 7219 866 8
ISBN 978 0 299 34194 7

This book is available in a digital edition

Library of Congress Cataloging-in-Publication
data is available

Published with the generous support of
the Aarhus University Research Foundation,
the Nordic Council of Ministers, and the
Danish Arts Foundation

The Nordic World series is copublished by
Aarhus University Press and the University
of Wisconsin Press

All rights reserved. Except for the quotation
of short passages for the purpose of criticism
and review, no part of this publication may
be reproduced, stored in a retrieval system,
or transmitted, in any form or by any means,
without the prior permission of the publishers

Aarhus University Press
aarhusuniversitypress.dk

The University of Wisconsin Press
uwpress.wisc.edu

Contents

Chapter 1.
Introduction 7

Chapter 2.
The Nordic energy mix 12

Chapter 3.
The early energy systems, 1850–1945 35

Chapter 4.
The great acceleration 47

Chapter 5.
Nordic energy in a wider world 65

Chapter 6.
Infrastructures and markets 75

Chapter 7.
Nuclear power 93

Chapter 8.
Conclusions 105

Chapter 1.
Introduction

Energy is a crucial factor for human survival. With the industrial revolutions, energy became indispensable to the constant and ongoing modernization of production and everyday life – for better and for worse. However, the use and significance of energy are also constantly changing, as recent historical events have made abundantly clear. The rapid economic recovery and growth following the paralytic parenthesis of the COVID-19 pandemic and in particular the Russian invasion of Ukraine have disrupted energy markets, most notably the gas market, leading to soaring energy prices. These developments made energy mean something very different in 2022 than it did in 2021. It has become evident to most people that energy is a limited and unevenly available resource, and one that is frequently linked to geopolitical conflicts. We have also learned that higher energy prices can be a social problem, even while advantageously affecting climate policies and accelerating the green transition.

We have seen these scenarios before. In the past, restricted and unstable supplies have challenged the security of supply,[1] due to conflicts in authoritarian states and attempts to use energy as a political means to encourage other nations to support certain views. Over time, wars

[1] The term "security of supply" refers to a high degree of certainty in the ongoing, uninterrupted provision of adequate volumes of a necessary basic resource, examples being food, water, and electricity

and conflicts have made energy a tangible, material aspect of life, both on the political agenda and for ordinary citizens around the globe, but our perceptions of energy have also continuously changed.

For many years the debate about the impact of energy systems on Earth's environment and climate has highlighted the negative aspects of energy.[2] It has also, therefore, changed the focus of energy history. Up until the mid-twentieth century the focus was on enthusiastic descriptions of technical progress, with countries constantly improving and expanding the gas and power production apparatus and the networks supplying their local communities. Then the focus shifted, and critical researchers began delving into large technical systems, analyzing the entanglement of technology and society, and the pros and cons of modernizing communities. In the context of this book, this shift signaled the ongoing changes in how people live their lives in relation to different energy regimes – for instance, the fossil fuel regime. In the new millennium, and especially in the last few years, sustainability has come to be a determining choreography in the historical understanding of energy.

It has become obvious that the energy mix and the design of energy systems, such as the gas and electricity grids in individual countries, are decisive for how a society can develop. What people and bodies decide energy systems issues? How is energy produced, and why? How is it distributed to consumers? How is it used in different countries and cultures? How can it be a decisive element in a geopolitical conflict that hinges on other issues? And what does the energy mix of tomorrow look like – and the energy systems of the future?

Each of the five Nordic countries has its own answers to these questions. The dissimilarities are due not only to geographical and climatic differences, but also to differences in opportunities, conditioned by each coun-

2. An "energy system" covers all activities related to the production, transmission, and distribution of energy

3. "Path dependence" refers to the way previous steps leading to an event or situation continue to influence how things develop in the future. Once a course has been chosen, certain steps will follow more naturally than others. This is particularly prevalent in infrastructure development, where sunk costs and existing built structures often obstruct new paths

try's economic, political, and cultural context. There is a good deal of path dependence here,[3] and a historical overview is necessary when seeking to understand these differences, in relation to both how the energy systems look today and where they are heading.

Although energy is one of the many areas where there is no "Nordic model", there are certain similarities between the five countries – Sweden, Norway, Finland, Denmark, and Iceland – or at least between the four countries on the European continent. Rather than a Nordic model, we find a common political-cultural notion that the Nordic countries can play a positive and innovative role in the green transition, due to the abundant presence of renewables, hydropower, wind power, and geothermal energy, and thanks to the unique potential they have to complement each other.

Furthermore, the Nordic energy systems are more or less integrated in several regional networks. Although the energy mixes are still subject to decisions made by the national parliaments, connections and interconnectedness have long been buzzwords in European energy policy and planning. The energy infrastructures and energy markets of European countries are becoming increasingly interwoven, and as of 2023 the ongoing energy crisis has emphasized the need for common and coordinated initiatives.

All five Nordic countries are already transitioning to greener energy, to a greater or lesser degree. Their transition paths differ because of each country's climate, geography, and history – where historical decisions, successes, and mistakes play a key role. Our intention is therefore to show how the energy infrastructures in these five countries have been planned and constructed differently over time, and how the systems act and interact in the regional context, which, to a growing extent, is defined by European cross-border cooperation.

More specifically, we aim to explain the current Nordic energy mix and its historical roots, going back to the introduction of modern energy systems in the nineteenth century, which includes the breakthrough of fossil fuels. The emerging systems created a path dependence based upon a quest for security of supply, combined with a notion of abundant energy that was used to modernize production and ways of living. In that sense, the great acceleration that took place in the decades immediately following World War II played a crucial role in creating energy-intensive societies (Nye 2001), based on fossil fuels and the expansion of activities that they enabled. This development changed and re-designed energy systems, as well as the daily lives of most people living in the Nordic countries.

A crucial aspect of these changes is the influence that energy-system transformation had in all five countries on their developing welfare states. Different political and planning frameworks have formed all five systems, particularly after the first oil crisis in 1973-1974, and even more so in recent years as they have moved towards green transitions. In this policy-driven shaping of the energy supply, state-owned energy companies are important actors, often in collaboration with local actors. We will therefore explain these energy systems as part of a global market on the one hand, and as a determining factor in day-to-day living and evolving Nordic lifestyles post-1900 on the other.

This book thus presents an overview of the historic and current energy systems in the Nordic countries, focusing on the role of these systems in a larger world and also in a local household context. In Chapter 2 we present the existing energy mixes in the five Nordic countries, as well as various structural challenges for each system. Note that here we deal with the five energy systems individually, whereas in subsequent chapters they are treated as a greater whole with different parts and trajectories, depending on geography, climate, cultural traditions, and so forth.

The next two chapters are historical, delving into the development and path dependencies of the different systems. Chapter 3 traces the early development of gas and electricity networks, laying the foundations of energy use and governance at the turn of the nineteenth century. In Chapter 4 we follow the great acceleration after World War II, with its proliferation of fossil fuel systems and the societal and cultural changes this entailed. One resulting change was greater import dependency. Accordingly, Chapter 5 discusses how import and energy security issues have played out differently across the five countries. Chapter 6 looks in greater detail at the relations between states and markets, describing the break with public monopolies and some of the most influential energy companies in each country. In Chapter 7 we discuss nuclear power, an energy source that has been of central importance to some Nordic countries while being completely rejected by others. Finally, our conclusions in Chapter 8 outline some of the challenges the Nordic countries face as they strive to complete their transitions to sustainable energy systems and behaviors.

Chapter 2.
The Nordic energy mix

The Nordic countries are sometimes described as "a model with five exceptions," which certainly applies to their energy sectors, both historically and today. The nations in the Nordic region – which actually encompasses five countries and three self-governing territories[4] – may have inspired each other, but ultimately their five mainland energy sectors are quite different in most respects. The energy sources they use differ greatly, and the level of personal energy use is much higher in Iceland and Norway than in the other three countries (Figure 2.1 and Figure 2.2). This is due to climatic conditions and available resources, but also to political decision-making and economic strategies.

On the other hand, the five energy systems have a shared backdrop: the global energy market. The oil crises of the 1970s played a crucial role in defining this context. The first crisis, which centered on Western relations with oil-producing Middle Eastern countries, resulted in an oil embargo and an ensuing severe constriction of oil availability, as well as a quadrupling of oil prices. This oil crisis led to greater volatility in the global oil market and paved

4.
In alphabetical order: Denmark, the Faroe Islands and Greenland (with these three constituting the joint Kingdom of Denmark); Finland (including Åland); Iceland; Norway; and Sweden

the way for a growing awareness of energy as a limited resource, and of consumption control as an urgent task. The overall problem was to decouple energy use from economic growth. This could be done in several ways, but energy conservation and more efficient utilization were two obvious options, which were therefore used in all the Nordic countries, to varying degrees. All five countries met the decoupling target, with Iceland achieving this ten years later than the others. This probably made for a smoother introduction of renewable energy sources into the existing energy infrastructures, but it did not contribute to solving the fundamental problems related to fossil fuel consumption in other sectors.

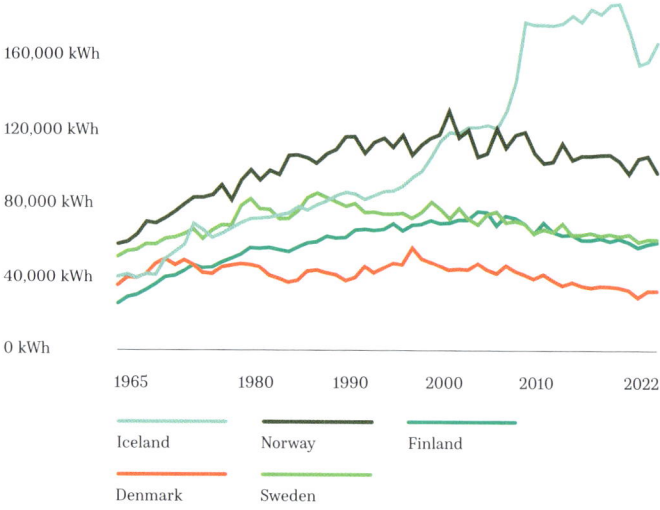

Figure 2.1 Per capita energy consumption in the Nordics

Source: Global Carbon Budget (2023); Population based on various sources (2023)

Sweden's energy mix

While Sweden is a country rich in natural resources such as forests, waterfalls, and certain minerals, it has not been blessed (or cursed) with fossil fuels to any significant extent. This is clearly mirrored in the Swedish energy mix, which is based, on the one hand, on domestic electricity production and, on the other, on imported fuels, which make up roughly 60% of Sweden's total annual energy input (in the form of uranium/nuclear fuel, oil and petroleum products, coal, biofuels, and some electricity) (Kaijser & Högselius 2019), some of which is inevitably lost in trans-

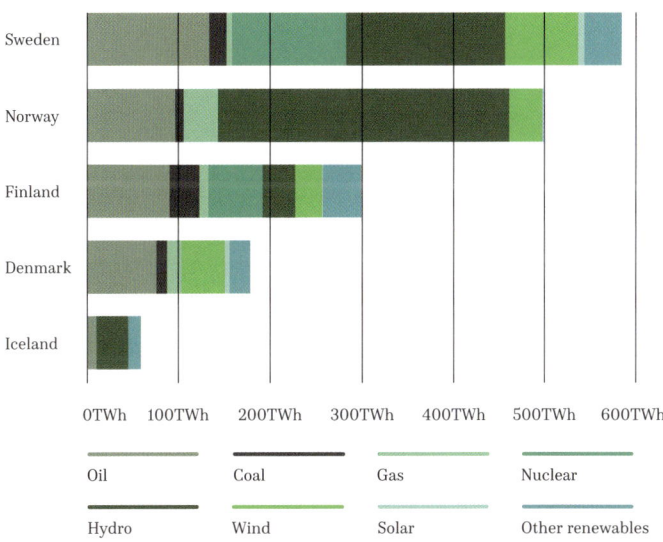

Figure 2.2 Primary energy consumption in the Nordics by source, 2023

Source: Energy Institute - Statistical Review of World Energy (2023)

mission, transfer, and other non-energy-use processes. In addition, the main heavy industries of historical national importance in Sweden are energy intensive. Examples are paper and pulp, mining, and steel production. A case in point is that in the industrial sector, just over 50% of the energy consumed goes into the paper and pulp industry. Furthermore, the climates of the Nordic countries generally make heating a central component of their energy consumption, and Sweden is no exception.

The total use of energy[5] in Sweden has stayed on a level of roughly 500-600 TWh since the 1980s, peaking in the early 2000s, and decreasing slightly since the 2010s, despite a population increase of more than 2 million people since 1980 (Swedish Energy Agency statistics database 2022). This general stagnation is one result of the above-mentioned decoupling of energy use and economic growth, and it came as a surprise for the utility companies and politicians, who had previously projected increased energy use, especially in terms of electricity. The decreases over the last couple of years have largely come from the industry and transport sectors, mainly as a result of energy efficiency measures. Besides this, the characteristics of new industrial developments make them less energy intensive than legacy industries.

A closer look at the different uses of energy in Sweden reveals that the dominant energy carrier is electricity. Hydropower has been the steady baseline electricity provider in the Swedish system, remaining at about 40% since it reached its peak development in the early 1970s. Nuclear power developed quickly over the 1970s, reaching its peak development in the mid-1980s. Since then it has consistently produced another roughly 40% of Sweden's electricity, although the share has recently diminished following the decommissioning of several nuclear reactors. Thus, in 2020 and 2021, hydropower increased its share to about 45% of the supply, with nuclear power supplying about 30%. Wind power is growing fast, and currently accounts for 16-17% of electricity production. The remaining production consists of 1% solar power along with inciner-

5. Including transmission losses and non-energy use. In this book, large-scale energy volumes are referred to in the units TWh (terawatt-hour), kWh (kilowatt-hour), PJ (petajoule), and GJ (gigajoule)

ation-based industries and co-generation plants (Swedish Energy Agency ET 2022:09).

Most of this electricity is used for housing and in the service sector (including agriculture and public institutions). Heating is the main use for this segment, with electric heating being the most common model for small houses, while district heating is more common in apartment buildings. The second-largest user of electricity is the industrial sector, notably the paper and pulp industry. A small but growing part of electricity consumption is used in the transport sector, a trend that is expected to continue. Sweden also had net electricity exports to its neighboring countries of 25 TWh in 2020, which increased to 34 TWh in 2022; the country is a net exporter of electricity to Denmark and Finland, and a net importer from Norway.

District heating[6] is another important energy carrier in Sweden, covering 59% of the total energy used to heat homes and water in 2020. The district heating system expanded slowly but steadily from the 1950s onwards, before stagnating in recent years. Now (as of 2021), the system is dominated by biofuels, which supply 65% of its needs, while a mix of other fuel types (such as natural gas, excess heat, heat pumps, petroleum products, and waste) account for the remaining 35% (Swedish Energy Agency statistics database 2022).

Biofuels generally account for quite a large share of Sweden's total energy input. This category includes raw and refined wood products as well as liquid biofuels, for example bioethanol, biodiesel, and biogas. Such fuels are used in a plethora of fields, such as heating – both directly in individual homes and in district heating systems – electricity production, and transport. However, biofuels are mainly used in district heating and industrial processes, which together make up 68% of total biofuel consumption.

6.
In a district heating system, entire towns or neighborhoods are interconnected with a common pipe network, distributing heat generated at a central boiler station or in a central combined heat and power (CHP) generation plant

The next major energy carrier in terms of usage is grouped as oil and petroleum products. Since the 1970s the use of fossil fuels in the Swedish energy system has dropped by more than 50%, mainly due to the substitution of oil heating with electric heating from nuclear power, but also because of efficiency measures put in place after the oil crisis. Most petroleum products are used in the transport sector, but a small part is also used for industry and heating, and for machines in the service sector. Heating is the sector where the use of petroleum products has decreased the most over the past 40 years. As for other fossil fuels, coal and natural gas are used in relatively small amounts, chiefly for industrial processes.

In Sweden (as in Norway, Finland, and Denmark), gross energy consumption has been steady for several decades, with a slight decrease in all sectors (transport,

Figure 2.3 Energy consumption by source, Sweden

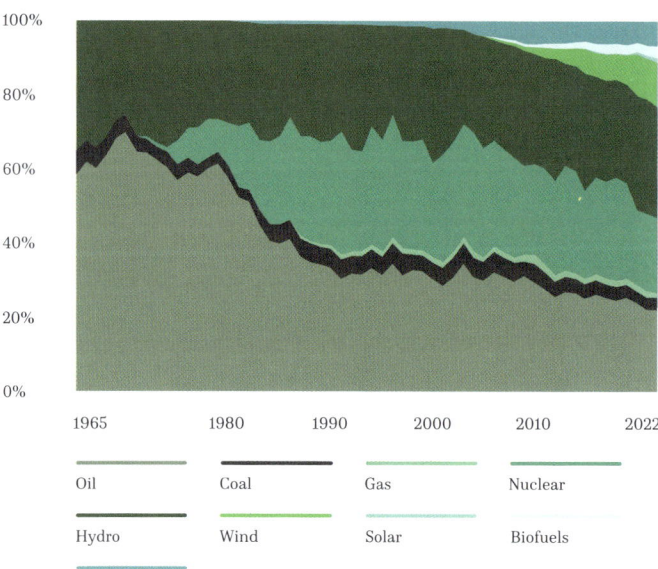

Oil   Coal   Gas   Nuclear
Hydro   Wind   Solar   Biofuels
Other renewables

Source: Energy Institute - Statistical Review of World Energy (2023)

housing and services, and industry). It is worth noting that during the years of global economic crisis in 2008–2009, energy consumption fell to a level not seen again until 2019, swiftly surging back in 2010 to pre-crisis levels, then declining slightly over the years until once again reaching "crisis level" around 2019. Trends observable over the past decades include a steady increase in biofuels (usage has tripled over the past 30 years) and wind power, coupled with a long-term, slow decrease in the use of fossil fuels. Solar power is also increasing, especially in recent years, rising from 0.4% to 1.1% of Swedish electricity generation between 2019 and 2021.

Norway's energy mix

Norway is one of the few countries in the world with abundant resources of both hydropower and fossil fuels, the latter made available following the discovery of rich oil and natural gas fields in the North Sea in the late 1960s. In just a few decades, Norway achieved energy independence and became the world's third-largest exporter of fossil fuels. These circumstances meant the country was able to choose which path to pursue in terms of its national energy mix. Hydropower, which today accounts for more than 90% of electricity production and 65% of energy consumption in Norway, took off after World War II and has been increasing ever since. In the last five years, substantial investment has increased the production of wind power, which now accounts for 9% of electricity consumption. Today renewables are the preferred energy source because they meet the demand for carbon-free energy production, and they cover more than 70% of energy use. Oil and natural gas, on the other hand, account for 20% and 10%, respectively, of Norwegian energy consumption; it is interesting to note that the share of fossil fuels in the country's gross energy consumption has been almost constant since the first oil crisis in 1973.

Norway is one of the most energy-hungry countries in the world (Our World in Data). In 2021, it consumed 568 TWh, and each Norwegian used 104,000 kWh of energy, 29,000 kWh of this in the form of electricity. Although energy consumption is high in actual numbers, Norwegian greenhouse gas emissions per capita are the second lowest in the Nordics because of all the hydropower in the energy mix. Per capita CO_2 emissions are still relatively high, however, due to the country's aluminum production (Our World in Data).

In 2020, the manufacturing sector accounted for 37% of the total energy consumption, but as in most other sectors (but not in agriculture, fishing, or construction), electricity was the main carrier of energy (Figure 2.4). The impact of the manufacturing sector is shrinking, due to structural changes and better energy efficiency. Transport and households accounted for 22–24% of total energy consumption. Several incentives, including a well-functioning and expanding vehicle charging infrastructure, have meant that the number of electric vehicles (EVs) has mushroomed, and four out of every five new cars sold today are EVs. Biofuels are the second-largest energy source for heating in Norwegian households (Energy Facts Norway; hydropower.org).

Norway's offshore fields contain huge amounts of oil and natural gas, and the country has been self-sufficient in fossil fuels since the 1980s. On land, water is another crucial resource, as most of the electricity produced in Norway is hydropower, and when needed Norway exports hydropower to Sweden and Denmark. A third of the country is covered in forest. Although this is much less forest than there is in either Finland or Sweden and the forested areas are shrinking, it is enough to fulfil the domestic demand for biomass.

After rising steeply in the 1990s, gross domestic energy consumption has only increased slightly over the last

Figure 2.4 Energy consumption by source, Norway

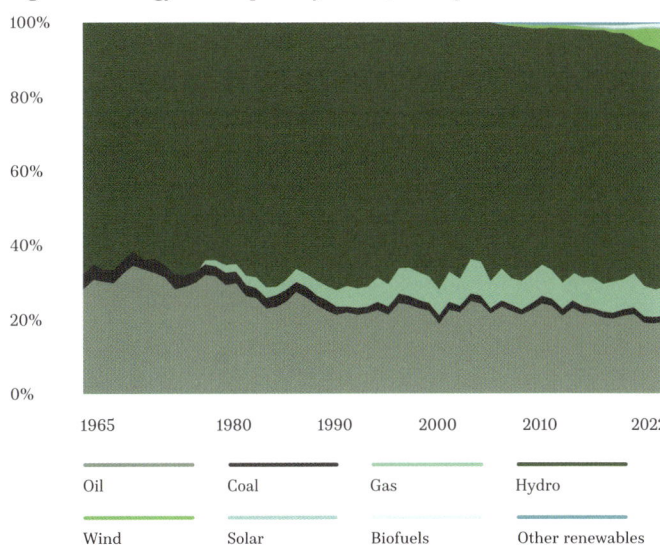

Source: Energy Institute - Statistical Review of World Energy (2023)

20 years, with a small decline after 2017–2019. In 2021, the total energy use was 568 TWh. Electricity covers a larger share of consumed energy than in most other European countries, since most of Norway's heating and industrial processes use it. As 90% of the electricity is hydropower and most of the rest is wind power, the energy system is substantially greener than in most European countries.

District heating and gas have gained ground in recent years, but they still supply only a little more than 10% of heating needs. Electricity dominates the energy use in industry, the service sector, and households, while oil-based products are most important in transport.

Industry and transport are the two most energy-consuming sectors, followed by services and households, while the other sectors use only small amounts of energy (Energy Facts Norway). In industry and mining, electricity makes up 64% of the energy used. This is because Norway's aluminum production is largely based on processes that only use electricity. The abundance of hydropower has allowed this industry to thrive, and the combined output from seven companies has made Norway the largest aluminum producer in Europe. Aluminum is an extremely energy-intensive commodity because of the high temperatures required to make it. The production of other metals and chemical products combines the use of electricity with gas and coal, while wood processing primarily uses biomass combined with electricity.

As in other countries, in Norway structural changes have led to lower industrial energy consumption, as energy-intensive production facilities have been replaced by more efficient factories or less energy-intensive production lines. Overall, the bottom line shows an increase in the use of electricity, district heating, and gas, and a decrease in the use of coal and oil.

Households consume approximately 22% of the country's energy use, or 171 PJ. The share of this provided by electricity is growing and has now reached about 80% (2021) due to greater use of electrical appliances and the phasing out of fossil fuels in heating. The household sector uses some 70–80% of its energy on heating. Second to electricity, bioenergy (especially biomass) covers a substantial part of the energy used for heating in Norway, while oil only accounts for a small part of this. However, the mix of energy carriers producing heat is changing. Since 2000, Norwegians have invested in more than a million heat pumps, and district heating has more than quadrupled, with each technology producing approximately 21 PJ (Statistics Norway).

The entire transport sector represents one quarter of the country's energy consumption. This mirrors the picture throughout the Nordics: most of the oil products a country uses go into transport. But as mentioned, EVs are gaining ground. In 2022 more than 500,000 were plying

Norway's roads, and consequently the amount of energy consumed by cars has gone down in recent years.

Denmark's energy mix

Denmark has the second-lowest per capita CO_2 emissions in the Nordics. Back in the mid-1990s the Danish level was much higher than those of the other Nordic countries, but emissions have since been reduced by two thirds.

As in many other countries, coal and oil once dominated the market in Denmark, but its responses to the two oil crises in the 1970s made room not only for natural gas but also for renewables – and in notoriously windswept Denmark, "renewables" primarily means wind power. As early as the 1980s, the Danish wind industry proved that renewables had a future, at least if they were subsidized by the state. Against this backdrop, and bolstered

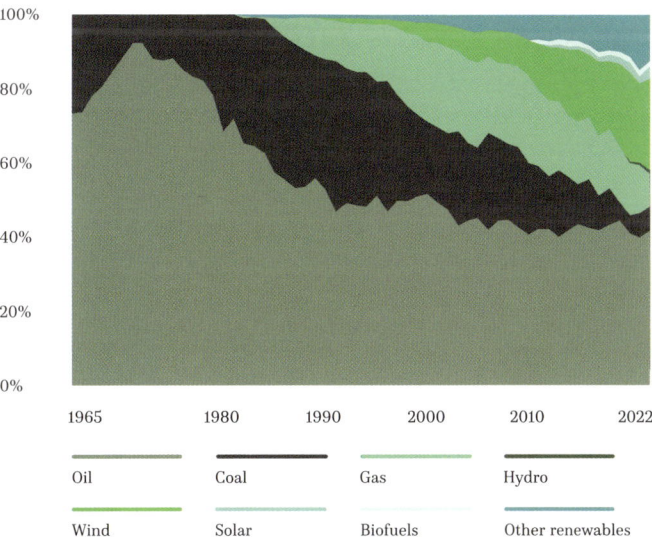

Figure 2.5 Energy consumption by source, Denmark

Source: Energy Institute - Statistical Review of World Energy (2023)

by subsidies, a history of entrepreneurship, organizational experiments, EU directives translated into national legislation, and efficiently run companies helped to transform Denmark's energy mix and move it in a more sustainable direction.

If we look at the current energy mix, it is clear that while it is still based on fossil fuels, a shift away from fossil fuels is under way, signaling the end of an era. Nevertheless, among the Nordic countries, Denmark has the second-smallest share of renewables, with only Finland trailing further behind.

In 2021 the gross energy consumption amounted to 673 PJ, of which oil accounted for 40% and natural gas for 9%. This equals 115 GJ per capita. Oil consumption has been fairly constant since 2010. In contrast, the consumption of renewables has increased since 1990, especially in the electricity sector, rising from 6% of gross energy consumption to 35%. Of this 35%, wind power makes up more than half of the power generated. There is, however, an ongoing use of fossil fuels, especially coal, as the stabilizing element, together with biomass, which is defined as a CO_2-neutral fuel. The current global crisis, which is causing a reduced output of energy and soaring demand, reveals that coal and gas are used during peak hours and to meet the higher demand. Danish power stations faced serious problems when required to reduce their use of coal even while ensuring the security of supply during the most recent energy crisis, and Denmark therefore decided to halt its phasing out of coal (Danish Energy Agency, DEA 2019; Our World in Data).

Unlike the other Nordic countries, Denmark has few natural resources, except for some oil and natural gas fields in the North Sea. Accordingly, it has traditionally had very few energy-intensive industries, with cement production as the most notable exception. The Danish offshore fields are not nearly as rich and productive as the Norwegian ones. Still, they were ample enough to take Denmark from being completely dependent on imported fossil fuels to becoming self-sufficient from 1997 to 2012 – the only country in the European Union to do so. In addition, Denmark was a net exporter of oil and natural gas from 1993 to 2018, and it is still a net exporter of natural gas.

In 2021, transport and households accounted for 31% of gross energy consumption, while industry and agriculture accounted for 22%, commerce and public services for 14 %, and non-energy uses for 2% (Danish Energy Authority, DEA).

The dominant energy carrier is electricity, 52% of which was provided by wind power in 2021. The rest is primarily produced by co-generation plants based on imported biomass, biogas, and coal, as well as natural gas from the North Sea.

Electricity is used in households, services, and production, which each account for approximately one third of the total usage. In the first two of these sectors electricity use is increasing, while it is declining in industrial production. Denmark's import and export of electricity fluctuates year on year, depending on weather conditions, prices on the Nordic spot market, Nordpool, and other varying factors. In 2021 the country imported a small amount of power from Sweden and Norway (40 PJ) and exported an even smaller amount to Germany and the Netherlands (22 PJ).

Most of the thermal power[7] is co-generated with heat, covering a fifth of the country's total energy consumption. The use of district heating took off in the early 1960s, but – as in Sweden – this technology has reached stagnation and perhaps even declined slightly in recent years, probably due to greater focus on heat pumps. Biomass (wood, wood pellets, straw, and the like) has become the "new oil" and its use has doubled (to 80 PJ in 2020) since 2012. More than half of this biomass is imported, pri-

7.
"Thermal power" is electricity generated by heat turbines

8.
https://www.dst.dk/da/Statistik/nyheder-analyser-publ/bagtal/2019/2019-11-14-Danmark-producerer-rekord-meget-biomasse-og-mere-af-det-kommer-fra-importeret-trae

marily from the Baltics, the US, Canada, and Russia.[8] Finland and Sweden burn more biomass than Denmark, but these two countries have vast forest resources on which to base their biomass use. The use of biofuels and especially biogas in Denmark has increased dramatically since 2010, due to large subsidies, although the extent to which biofuels are CO_2 neutral is debatable.

The Kingdom of Denmark includes two self-governing territories: Greenland and the Faroe Islands. Although this book will focus on the mainland territories, it is valuable to point out some main trends in these territories as well. Electricity production in Greenland has changed profoundly over the last 15 years. Hydropower has taken over as the main energy source and now accounts for 83% of power consumption (2021), while the use of oil has been halved and covers the remaining consumption. Thus, the increase in electricity consumption has been met with hydropower. Accordingly, the main energy company in Greenland, Nunaoil, decided to change its strategy to focus on renewables in 2022, also changing its name to NunaGreen. This is a limited company owned by the government of Greenland (Nukissiorfiit; nunagreen.gl). In 2021, Greenland used 9.258 TJ[9] in total, with the energy sector and manufacturing industry being the two most energy-consuming sectors (StatBank Greenland).

9. 1 TJ (terajoule) = 0.001 PJ

In contrast to most countries in Europe, the Faroe Islands continue to increase their dependence on oil, which is used for electricity production, for heating, and in the transport sector. The power supply across the 18 islands in this North Atlantic archipelago is divided into seven isolated power systems. Since 2015 the share of oil in electricity production has increased from 42% to 62%, while hydropower has decreased from 39% to 26% and wind from 19% to 12%. However, following the inauguration of a new wind farm in 2021, wind and hydropower will account for a larger share of future electricity production in the Faroes (SEV).

Finland's energy mix

Among the Nordic countries, Iceland and Finland have historically been behind the region's curve of stagnating energy consumption. These are the two countries that have increased their energy consumption the most per capita since 1990, albeit total energy use in Finland peaked in the 2010s and has since decreased slightly.

In terms of total energy use, nearly half goes to Finland's industrial sector. Like Sweden, Finland has energy-intensive industries in forestry, including paper and pulp production, and also in steel production. The remaining

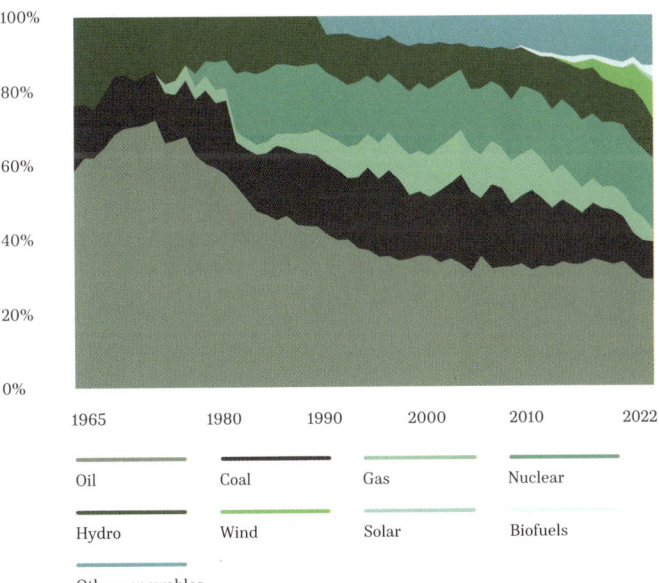

Figure 2.6 Energy consumption by source, Finland

Source: Energy Institute - Statistical Review of World Energy (2023)

half of the energy consumed is almost equally distributed among transportation, homes, and services.

The total consumption is dominated by electricity and oil, with direct use of biofuels and district heating as other significant elements. Finland has significant national biofuel production, which accounts for most of the country's domestic energy production. This, in turn, has made it a leader in research into, and development of, biofuels, especially biodiesel.

Finland, like Sweden and Iceland, lacks fossil fuels of its own, so all three countries depend on imports for much of their total energy input. Slightly less than 50% of Finland's total primary energy supply is imported. Most of this has historically come from Russia, which makes the nature of the Finno-Russian relationship different from Russia's relations with the other Nordic countries. We will return to the historic reasons for this in Chapter 5. Up until the Russian invasion of Ukraine in February 2022, Russia was Finland's sole supplier of natural gas, and its chief supplier of oil and coal. Nuclear fuel for one of Finland's two nuclear power plants also comes from Russia. However, from the first quarter to the third quarter of 2022, pipeline imports of natural gas from Russia to Finland plummeted from 308 million cubic meters to 0, and electricity imports from Russia were also completely cut off. Finnish imports of Russian coal and most oil products also dropped by more than half (Statistics Finland 2022). This has partly been compensated for by an increase in crude oil imports from Norway, and electricity imports from Norway and Sweden.

Generally, the use of fossil fuels in the Finnish energy system has decreased since the 2010s, while the share of renewable energy has increased. Oil makes up the largest share of fossil fuels, and while oil is used to some degree in all of the various sectors, it completely dominates the transport sector, covering 94% of transport consumption. While the use of oil has been slowly declining, mainly in heating, the greatest decrease over the past decade has taken place in the supply of coal, natural gas, and peat. These fuels are mainly used for power and heat generation, but natural gas consumption, for instance, has declined by half between 2006 and 2019, shrinking further during 2022 and now only representing 2.8% of total Finnish energy consumption (Statistics Finland 2022). Overall, except in transport, most sectors in Finland show considerable diversity in their fuel consumption and energy carriers.

In the electricity system, nuclear power is the main source, followed by hydropower and imported electricity, mainly from Sweden. Together these sources provide around 70% of the electricity supply (Statistics Finland 2022). The remainder is covered by combined heat and power (CHP) plants (which use diverse fuels, such as biofuels, coal, and natural gas) and some wind power, along with a small amount of solar power. Electricity consumption is shared more or less evenly between housing and services on the one hand and the industrial sector on the other, with forestry and the chemical industry as the largest users by far.

As in the other Nordic countries, heating is an important market in Finland, and district heating provides about half of all space heating. Biofuels and peat make up at least one third of the fuel gathered for use in the district heating system, especially in northern and central Finland. In the coastal areas, coal and natural gas are more widely used.

Peat holds a special place in the Finnish energy system, and within the EU, Finland is second only to Ireland in the share of peat used in its energy supply. As categories go, peat belongs with fossil fuels and is therefore among the energy sources currently being phased out. However, historically peat has played an important political role in

Finland, and it remains an important fuel source for heat and power plants today.

Finland's gross annual total consumption of energy peaked in the early 2000s and has since slightly decreased, staying relatively stable during the 2010s. The largest decreases in consumption after 2010 were in the industrial sector and space heating.

Iceland's energy mix

Today, Iceland's annual per capita consumption of energy is one of the highest in the world, at approximately 170,000 kWh (Our World in Data). One defining feature of the country's energy mix is that geothermal energy forms the backbone of the system, accounting for 55% of total consumption. Geothermal and hydropower combined make for an energy mix with 80% renewables. Geothermal power is mainly used for space heating, but it also accounts for 25% of electricity generation (National Energy Authority, NEA).

Hydropower use increased after World War II, followed by an increase in the use of geothermal power from the 1970s onwards. At the same time, imports of fossil fuels decreased: having covered some 50% of space heating needs around that time, 20 years later this percentage was negligible.

One reason for the growing electricity demand in Iceland is the rapid expansion of its aluminum industry and other energy-intensive industries, which account for 80% of its electricity consumption (NEA).

Of all the Nordics, Iceland also has the largest share of renewables – the above-mentioned 80% – in its energy system, thanks to the island nation's abundant geothermal energy and hydropower potential. The only fossil fuels used today are oil derivatives for the transport sector, but the use of gasoline is diminishing as EVs gain popularity.

The Icelandic climate has cool summers and often bone-chilling winters. For space heating, geothermal energy is the obvious first choice. Hydropower provides more than 70% of the country's electricity, with geothermal energy in second place. CHP plants and geothermal plants provide electricity, district heating, and hot water to most of the country. Thermal springs with hot water, and geysers with hot water and steam, are so abundant that the capital of Reykjavík is a sustainable city, and in many locations hot water can be tapped from city pipes without passing through a boiler or water heater.

This abundance of hydropower has nourished a growing manufacturing sector. Aluminum production is the most important industry to use land-based natural resources. Production began in 1969 and has been growing ever since, reaching more than 800,000 metric tons in 2020 and making Iceland an important global player on the aluminum market. This highly energy-intensive industry accounts for one third of the country's total CO_2 emissions, but since 2005 its emissions have been decreasing.

While the industrial sector uses 14% of Iceland's total energy consumption, the service sector is the most energy-consuming sector (35%), followed by households (23%). Once again space heating makes up a major part, some 60%, of household energy consumption, with fossil fuels – gasoil and diesel – accounting for about 25% and electricity for the remaining 15%.

Similarities and differences

After the first oil crisis in 1973-1974 the five Nordic countries took different approaches to the many fundamental changes taking place in their energy systems. Each had, and has, its own particular climate, resources, and history, as we shall see in the next chapters – which, for practical reasons, deal with the four continental European countries and to some extent Iceland. They do not address the energy systems in the three independent territories, which each have their own systems and challenges. Nevertheless, there are similarities worth pointing out, although they do not mean the countries underwent the same development simultaneously, or at the same pace. Rather, they highlight certain common features and trends.

During the Cold War, all five countries were oriented towards the West, with Sweden declared neutral and Finland forced to consider the interests of the then Soviet Union (USSR). This impacted their development after World War II, as we will see below. All five Nordics are also welfare states, which implies a relatively high energy consumption per capita and means that public institutions account for a sizable share of it, as well as that national and local governments set out rules and guidelines for this consumption. Thus, the five states have democratically entrenched tools to influence the energy mixes in their country, and also to change consumption based on environmental and climate considerations. Two key examples of this are the decoupling of energy consumption from economic growth, and the significant growth in renewable energy sources over the last 20 years. This restructuring of the energy mix has been helped along by climatic conditions, specifically regarding water and wind. The five countries also share their relatively cold climates, which makes heating a significant item in their national energy accounts. Furthermore, as in most other countries, transport poses a challenge as it is based on fossil fuels, and it has proved difficult to slow the growth in traffic and make it sustainable.

Despite these similarities, it is quite clear that the differences between Nordic energy systems are more pronounced. The five energy mixes and their respective histories are extremely different, due, for example, to existing resources (such as access to hydropower, or a lack of it) and to historical differences in each country's perception

Figure 2.7 Energy consumption by source, Iceland

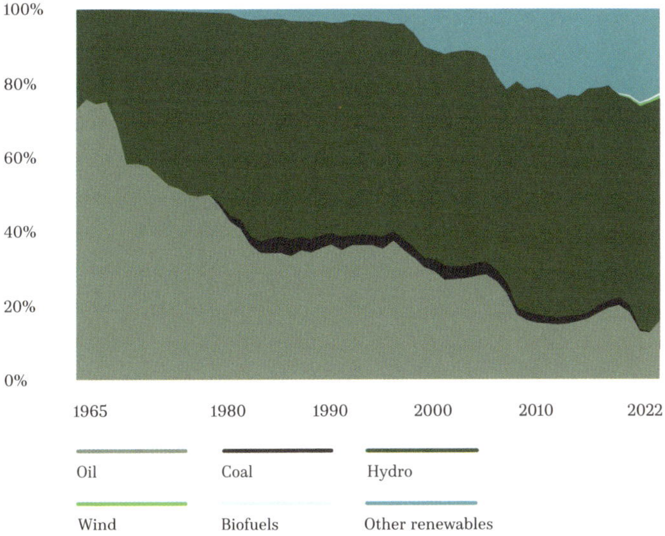

- Oil
- Coal
- Hydro
- Wind
- Biofuels
- Other renewables

Source: Energy Institute - Statistical Review of World Energy (2023)

of electricity's role in their ongoing modernization (where, for instance, Denmark has focused more on fossil fuels). The climate targets agreed in recent years have, however, created a consensus that electricity is an indispensable part of the future if the countries' goals are to be met.

All Nordic countries to some extent exhibit stagnating energy consumption, although Norway and Iceland are still at a level comparable to where they were in 1990 and show no declining trend. Meanwhile, if we look at the climate targets, all the Nordics have reduced their CO_2 emissions (Figure 2.8). Even so, it is somewhat surprising that the two countries with the largest share of renewables in their energy systems – Iceland and Norway – also have the largest carbon footprints. As Figure 2.8 only reflects production-based emissions, part of the explanation for this is the aluminum production in both of these countries.[10]

10.
Different statistics state different numbers for per capita CO_2 emissions

Figure 2.8 Per capita CO2 emissions in the Nordics

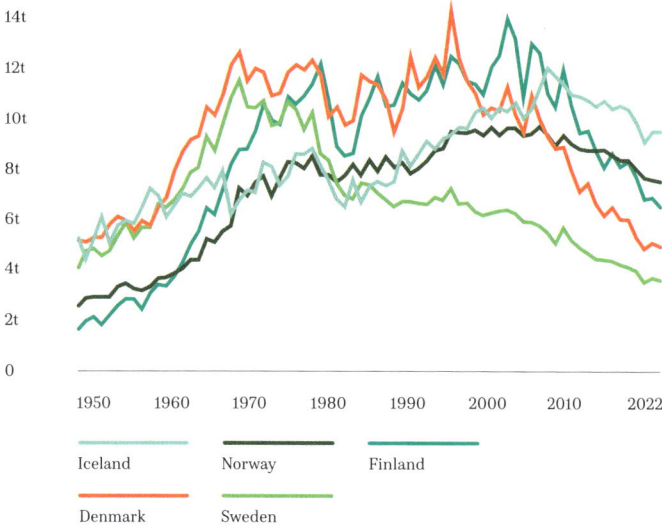

Source: Global Carbon Budget (2023); Population based on various sources (2023)

In addition to more use of renewables, improved energy efficiency is a crucial part of the overall reduction in CO_2 emissions, in the Nordic region and elsewhere, and in production as well as consumption. If the positive impact from these measures is to last and not be outweighed by increased consumption, there are many determining factors to consider, as discussed in the following chapters.

Chapter 3.

The early energy systems, 1850–1945

The breakthrough of gas

In most modern regions, from the mid-eighteenth century a succession of industrial revolutions fueled a transition away from pre-industrial societies, as their vulnerable energy balances were considered an obstacle to growth and to certain improvements in daily life.

One main reason why the industrial revolutions disrupted the whole world was that fossil fuels – primarily coal – quickly gained ground, initially in production. This was enabled by technological innovations, but another factor was the stability of coal as a fuel. Because it could be transported and stored, coal did not necessarily have to be used for production near the coal mine. What is more, fossil fuels were abundant in relation to the demand for them, though the latter was rapidly swelling. Even so, biomass remained an important part of energy systems well into the twentieth century, especially in those Nordic countries with extensive woodlands. In Finland in particular, the use of fossil fuel did not really take off until after World War II, and instead the country underwent a development sometimes referred to as "timber-based industrialization" (Myllyntaus 2011).

The steam engine allowed energy to be produced locally. The only network associated with steam energy production consisted of suppliers of coal and other raw materials, which had no infrastructure that tied them together except for existing transport networks.

Infrastructures developed during the second industrial revolution, when energy became available in a network that connected utility companies with end users, like factories and private homes. From the early nineteenth century, gas and subsequently electricity gained ground to provide lighting and power to factories and workshops.

England was the front runner of industrialization. By comparison the small Nordic economies were slow off the mark, taking decades to create industrial societies mainly fueled by coal. Coal gas was an English technology that spread across Europe. The breakthrough of what was initially called "town gas" was prompted by the desire for better lighting, but the network idea was quickly applied to other urban features. Technologically, town gas was a system consisting of a gasworks linked to a widely branching grid. Along with water and sewer systems, the pipes that carried gas to consumers became a new underground urban infrastructure that heralded the modern age.

The introduction of grid-based street lighting raised the issue of ownership. Street lighting was a task usually handled by the public sector, and the question of whether gasworks should be publicly or privately owned became a hot political topic.

At first, private ownership was the preferred model. The technology had largely spread to the Nordics through English companies investing in the construction of gas plants abroad, for instance in Denmark. In line with the *Zeitgeist*, many believed the state ought to interfere as little as possible in economic life, concentrating instead

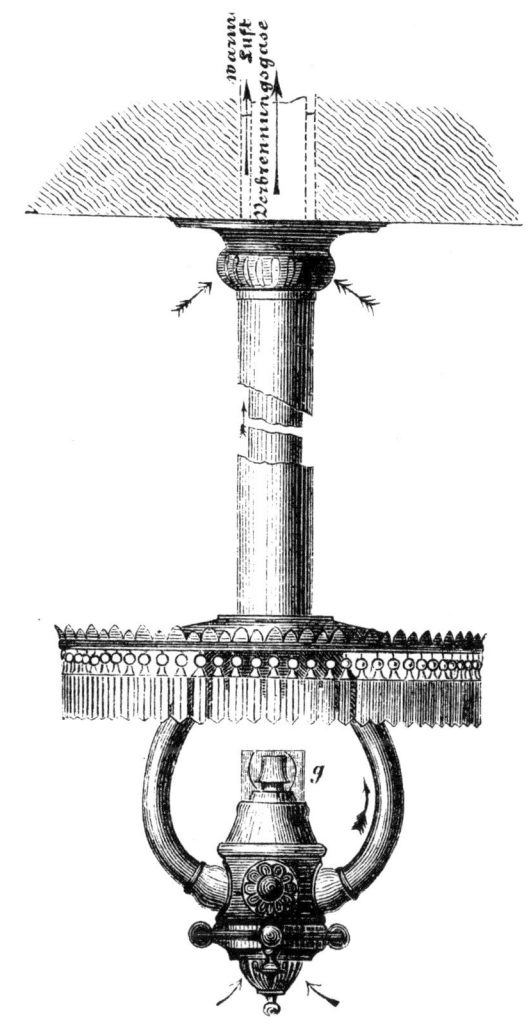

Gas lamp (1882)
Gas quickly moved indoors. Initially used for lighting the homes of well-to-do families, here in the ornamented style of the day, gas lamps soon became a common feature in ordinary homes too. © Quagga Media / Alamy Stock Photo

on the security of its citizens and their opportunities to engage in economic activity. Hence, providing well-lit streets was a public obligation, but very often a private gasworks served as the supplier. The local authorities quickly realized that here lay an opportunity for a stable income, in parallel with the improvements public utilities might offer in the security of supply. Compared to other countries the Nordic region's municipal authorities assumed ownership of the gas supply quite rapidly, doing so early in the twentieth century.

In Sweden and Denmark gas technology was an experimental field from around 1810, but some of the notable people in these efforts were rooted in Norway and Finland. In all four countries private gasworks were established in the 1840s and 1850s, primarily using coal as fuel, but also some kerosene and oil. Among the first to adopt the new technology were textile companies with ties to England (Hyldtoft 1995).

The first Nordic gasworks was commissioned in Gothenburg, Sweden, in 1846. Two years later the Norwegian capital of Christiania (modern-day Oslo) commissioned a gasworks, followed by the Swedish town of Norrköping and the capital of Stockholm in 1851 and 1853, respectively. In Denmark the first operational gasworks, located in Odense, went live in 1853. Over the next 10 to 15 years the four Nordic countries saw the number of gasworks rise dramatically, especially in Denmark, which soon had the densest coverage, and in Sweden.

The rapidly growing importance of gasworks must be seen in light of what, at the time, was a lack or limitation of national experience in constructing underground energy system grids. Copenhagen was the first Nordic capital to build and manage its own gas plant. The city's decision was motivated by three factors: Copenhagen would be able to reap the benefits of its own technological advances; profits would benefit local citizens, rather than a foreign company; and the project would give Danish technicians important training. A more theoretical argument was that the gas supply would be best and cheapest if it was handled as a "natural monopoly" under the auspices of the city (Hyldtoft 1995).

The local authority of Copenhagen discussed the gasworks issue for 13 years, and in 1857 the first gasworks was up and running. This coincided with a trend that saw public bodies or municipal authorities in the other Nordic countries also acting as the main driving force in building and managing gasworks. In 1870 about 50% of Swedish gasworks were municipal, while in Denmark it was about 80%. This probably indicates some kind of path dependence, reflecting the Danish tradition of stronger public presence in everyday life than was the case in Sweden.

As mentioned, gas lighting was first used outdoors in the streets, but it was soon introduced indoors as well, lighting factories, institutions, entertainment venues, major stores, and offices. This made evening and night shift work an option. Gas lighting also gradually gained ground in affluent private homes. It was a sign of luxury that slowly became mundane, and eventually gas was also used to light ordinary homes, although still competing with the kerosene lamp. Gas was also increasingly used for cooking (using gas burners and gas ovens) and for heating water, heating radiators, and powering certain small appliances such as irons. In production, gas became an important resource for small-scale manufactories and workshops, which could use gas to power small, inexpensive engines for their operations.

Electrification

Gas faced strong competition as electricity gained ground in the late nineteenth century. Electricity was a rival to the public gas supply, posing the obvious risk that if it was made available, electric power would reduce the municipal revenues from supplying gas. Against this backdrop it was only natural that private electricity operators with their own generator facilities came to play an important role in the introduction of electricity in the Nordics. The dominant technology was small thermal or hydropower generator stations, which did not require large investments (Thue 1995). The biggest hurdle was therefore the concession conditions set by the municipal authorities, which often reflected mixed feelings towards this new energy form. Such conditions could be quite strict, for example in Copenhagen, which decided on a more restrictive version of the concession conditions stipulated in Berlin (Thomsen & Thorndahl 2007).

The history of electric power in the Nordic countries began in the 1880s with small power stations of limited range, as the product was direct current. Notably, both the public sector and the industrial sector began to generate electricity, based either on coal (typically in urban settings) or, where possible, on hydropower – of which Denmark, unlike the other countries, had very little. In Norway the division between a large-scale industrial system and a system to supply the general public was more apparent than elsewhere (Högselius & Kaijser 2007). Some Danish and Swedish industrial companies also produced electricity for their own use. Likewise, some cities and towns produced electricity to operate their tram systems.

Quite early in the history of electricity in the Nordics, we see very different forms of production arising. As was the case with gas, electricity was first used for lighting, but soon it was also used to supply motive power to production lines. In Sweden and Norway rules for transmission were defined very early in the process, and until World War I these countries built out their national networks, in a few cases developing international branches. At the same time the public sector took on a greater role in the supply of electricity. In Sweden this resulted in regionalization and the founding in 1909 of the state-owned operator Vattenfall (the original Swedish name, meaning "the royal board of waterfalls", was later shortened to the word for "waterfalls"). In Norway, the state was directly involved in constructing power plants. In Denmark almost all power plants were either organized as cooperatives or municipally owned, and outside the capital region they were typically built in towns.

Early on, Sweden developed hydropower generation in or near modest industrial facilities and cities, mainly in the central and southern parts of the country. When the electricity grid expanded in the interwar period and it became possible to produce hydropower at greater distances from the industrial sites, most rivers in southern Sweden were developed, and the hydropower sector became structured through regional and municipal companies that were co-owned by the major industrial operators. Their primary goal was to produce cheap electricity, rather than large profits. Initially the industrial sector used 90% of the electricity Sweden produced, and having access to this cheap energy source improved its competitiveness. These early years were not without conflict, however. The development of hydropower dams affected lands and waters owned and used by farmers, and also attracted the attention of nature conservation groups. In addition, many people were against having dangerous high-voltage lines suspended over their properties. The laws were ultimately reworded, largely benefiting power companies and hydropower expansion (Jacobsson 1996; Kaijser & Högselius 2007).

The recession after World War I led to an overproduction of energy in Sweden, making it necessary to diversify the market. One new outlet came with the electrification of the Swedish railroad system; another was the growing electricity consumption of households. As in many other Western countries, Nordic power companies used propaganda and information campaigns about electricial household devices to encourage consumers, particularly housewives, to replace their wood and gas stoves with more expensive electrical appliances.

Nineteenth-century gas lamp
At first town gas or coal gas was mainly used for lighting the streets with lamps like this one, from the Nyboder quarter of Copenhagen. Most town dwellers saw this as progress and welcomed the improvement. Just 40–50 years later, gas lamps were replaced by electric streetlights. © Marshall Ikonography / Alamy Stock Photo

After most of the rivers in Sweden's southern regions had been developed, the next step was to develop the large rivers in the north, mostly situated in Sápmi, the transnational homelands of the indigenous Sámi peoples that stretch across the northern regions of Finland, Sweden, and Norway. This became possible through close technical collaboration between Vattenfall and ASEA, a private limited company, the aim being to develop high-voltage networks that could transport the electricity from the north to the south (Fridlund 1999). These networks became the first building blocks in a national network that Vattenfall was responsible for constructing. The national network enabled companies with different production contexts to buy from each other, as certain parts of the country generated less hydropower in some seasons and more in others. Although the first large-scale hydropower dam was built in the Stuor Julevädno/Grand Lule River as early as 1915, large-scale hydropower exploitation in the Finnish, Norwegian, and Swedish parts of Sápmi took place during the decades after World War II, culminating in the 1960s.

Hydropower was also the cornerstone of early electrification in Finland. Forestry played an especially crucial role in the development of the country's electricity grids. Up until the 1990s forestry and related businesses were the largest industrial segment in terms of manufacturing and exports, and because such operations are energy intensive, ensuring a supply of cheap, reliable energy sources was a central aim for industrialists there. Conventional wood fuel and new hydropower, the latter mostly arising from investments in the rivers of southern Finland, were the two main sources of electricity during the first half of the twentieth century. However, Finland lost a third of its hydropower capacity after World War II, as several plants were located in areas taken by the USSR. To replace this loss, and to meet a growing demand for electricity arising from the restructuring of the forestry industry, actors both public and private built hydropower plants in northern Finland and Sápmi during the 1940s and 1950s. By 1964 these efforts had increased Finland's hydropower capacity from 430 MW to 1925 MW (Myllyntaus 1991). This increase was used to meet the expanding needs of the industrial sector, especially paper production.

The large-scale development of hydropower in Sápmi provided electricity to power the industries and developing welfare states of Finland, Norway, and Sweden, as we will see in the following chapter. However, the expansion also meant a significant intervention in Sámi landscapes, leading, among other things, to fluctuating water levels and ice sheets, displacements, loss of cultural heritage sites, and the disruption of economic and cultural activities such as reindeer husbandry and fishing. Although over time Sámi groups increasingly became recognized as stakeholders in this development, the idea that large-scale hydropower was for the "common good" meant that the rights and interests of Sámi populations were generally ignored. Hydropower thereby became part and parcel of a longer history of colonialism and resource exploitation in Sápmi (Össbo 2018; Österin & Raitio 2020; Engen et al. 2023; Mustonen et al. 2010)

Two infrastructures

Thus, from the mid-nineteenth century until World War I, two infrastructures had emerged across the Nordics, most clearly in the cities and towns, signaling a new era for consumers. Not only had it become easier to replace darkness with light, it was also possible for homes – at least those in urban areas – to combine the two forms of energy. Both gas and power plants were established locally, on the initiative of industrious local individuals and private enterprises. It was often a challenge to get the plants up and running, and to keep them operating reliably, but the number of plants increased, and the electricity grid in particular continued to expand. This meant that slowly but surely, from being exclusive amenities for the well-off, gas and electricity became a necessary and integral part of everyday life, even in small towns.

During the interwar period, existing structures and systems were consolidated, but new trends also arose and were implemented. First, the geographical expansion of the power grids continued. The demand for electricity grew rapidly and was met by larger production units and an expansion of the networks for both transmission and distribution. After World War II, large-scale hydropower expansion in the north aided the development of Nordic industries and welfare states, while simultaneously furthering the colonial resource exploitation of Sápmi.

There was a growing need for capital, and stronger focus on efficiency. To meet these challenges, power producers began to think in terms of centralizing and concentrating production. The major electricity producers, be they private, cooperative, or public power stations, increasingly gained influence over, and control of, the networks. Unlike Sweden, Denmark remained divided into two separate electricity systems covering western and eastern Denmark, respectively. The grid in Norway was also divided in two, as the connections between the country's north and south were inadequate. Consequently, both countries established multiple price determination systems.

The same process did not apply to the gasworks, which technically had to operate with geographically limited distribution areas, even though they were just as diligent in streamlining production as the power plants. They also improved gas services for households. Especially in Denmark these two forms of energy were in competition, primarily in the kitchen. Modernist architects, who aimed to rationalize housing construction, were more interested in electricity than gas. The gas stove was probably better suited for cooking than the electric stove, but the electric kitchen was seen as "the future" – the way to give housewives an easier and less labor-intensive life. Electricity, the "clean" energy source, was a perfect fit for the clinical kitchens of the modern age. In addition, new products such as electric irons and vacuum cleaners had emerged, putting pressure on gasworks and gas appliance manufacturers to constantly reinvent themselves. On the other hand, gas cost less than electricity, and it was still the dominant household energy source in Denmark when World War II ended in 1945 and the country was liberated from occupation. From then on, however, the share of gas users began to shrink.

Before World War II, geography and available resources played a crucial role in constructing the early energy systems of the Nordic countries. For example, it was easier for a small country like Denmark to establish a national electricity system than it was for Sweden or Norway, despite these northerly neighbors' abundant hydropower resources. What is more, these new energy systems were socio-technical in that they relied not only on the building of infrastructures, but also on the creation of regulations, organizations, markets, and consumers, all of which would impact their future development. These first steps in energy-system building would prove to be decisive, as they established certain mindsets and path dependencies in each of the Nordic energy systems.

Chapter 4.
The great acceleration

The 1950s and 1960s have been described as a period of "great acceleration" in humanity's effect on Earth's ecosystems.[11] Many trends indicate that this impact increased significantly due to mass production and mass consumption. As the Nordic countries turned into affluent societies with energy-intensive lifestyles, they all contributed to these profound changes.

This lifestyle transformation is deeply interwoven with changes in energy systems. Like the rest of the Western world, the Nordic countries' pathway into the age of fossil fuels during the first industrial revolution was founded on coal, which was abundant and could be transported and stored. These three characteristics revolutionized the energy supply and turned it into a much more resilient system, not least because – as mentioned earlier – the sites of production and use no longer had to be located near each other.

After World War II, in many European countries coal came to be replaced by oil in heating, power generation, process energy, and transportation. This resulted in a high dependency on oil, mainly imported from the Middle

11. The concept of "the great acceleration" has been criticized for not taking into account the great geographical differences in global development during the twentieth century. Instead, the concept of "the great divergence" has been used to show diverging developments during this time. However, in terms of the Nordic countries, the former term is fitting (cf. Pomeranz 2000)

East, with the oil markets largely run by large oil companies referred to as "majors". Overall, the use of oil tripled, partly because oil is easier to handle than coal and partly because oil prices were low and even decreased during the 1960s (Pfister 2010). It has also been argued that the wish to avoid powerful coal unions played a role (Mitchell 2013). In addition, the American-initiated Marshall Plan, formally known as the European Recovery Program or ERP (1948–1952), aimed to help the war-ravaged countries of Europe get back on their feet after World War II by promoting the industrialization and rationalization of industry and agriculture.

Part of the ERP's growth policy was to help states subsidize more efficient and centralized energy systems based on coal and oil, in order to provide the energy needed to transform European societies. Cheap oil from the Middle East, delivered primarily by American companies (such as Standard Oil, Gulf, and Texaco) was meant to energize the world and make it a better place to live. To this aim, a crucial step was to improve productivity in both the agricultural sector and the industrial sector, transforming agriculture from manpower-based to machine-based production, and industry into a mass-production apparatus providing relatively cheap goods that were an indispensable part of what was promoted, at the time, as a "modern" lifestyle. The ERP therefore played a key role in the "oilification" of what, until then, had been coal-dominated societies in Western Europe, giving economic support for investments in oil-consuming products and supporting the development of refinery capacity (Painter 2009). Today, oil is still the most important fuel world-wide, covering more than a third of global energy consumption – and demand continues to increase.

Growth and demography

In the 1950s and onwards, the Nordic countries, like most of the Western world, saw strong GDP growth, partly based on a dynamic interrelationship between the private and public sectors. This also encompassed the development of national welfare systems and state support to develop infrastructures, as well as industrial innovation and production. In addition, the ERP helped the three Scandinavian countries (Sweden, Norway, and Denmark) to reduce problems with their national balances of payment, thus expanding their financial headroom to import foreign products. The five Nordic countries followed more or less the same economic trajectory, and they all opted to build welfare states.

Sweden, along with Norway, had been a leader in terms of GDP growth per capita between 1913 and 1950, largely due to the success of large exporting corporations and a thriving manufacturing sector. Having been spared warfare on its own territory in both world wars, Sweden came out of World War II with its cities and industries intact. This enabled established Swedish industrial and export companies to quickly resume operations, and there was a boom in the country's production of steel, communications equipment, and ball bearings, as well as in mining, shipbuilding, and the paper industry. In the first five years after the war Sweden had a GDP growth rate of nearly 5%. This, in tandem with a growing public service and welfare sector, led to higher employment rates, and to incoming waves of immigrant workers, particularly from Finland and, somewhat later, from Greece, Italy, and the Balkans (Sjögren in Fellman et al. 2008). Between 1950 and 1970, the Swedish economy exhibited a steady annual GDP growth rate of about 3%. As a consequence of the monetary crisis in the late 1960s, combined with the 1973 oil crisis, this growth would stagnate during the 1970s, staying at a level of 1.6% between 1974 and 1981.

Denmark saw varying growth rates until 1958, followed by a remarkable economic upswing. It was a latecomer in providing energy to industrial production, but in the late 1950s Danish industrial exports surpassed agricultural exports, indicating that the country was on its way to becoming an industrialized society. The industrial sector no longer produced primarily for the domestic market, and amid the global monetary liberalization, Denmark was accordingly exposed to international competition.

Imported oil spurred the mechanization of the agricultural sector. In all five countries tractors became a common sight in the countryside, while most of the draught horses disappeared. The use of milking machines and combine harvesters increased as well, and the quest for ever-more efficient cultivation methods paved the way for chemical fertilizers, which were used on an unprecedented scale (Meinander 2006). In addition, the mechanization of forestry was a key process taking place in Finland, Sweden, and Norway around this time.

Traditionally, forestry, fishery, and agriculture employed about 40% of the Norwegian population. However, industry became predominant after the country was liberated in 1945, and from the 1960s most new jobs were created in the public sector – with the consequence that 75% of the Norwegian workforce are in such jobs in 2020. Norway's economic growth was led by the government, which channeled huge investments into specific industries in order to further export-led growth. The aluminum industry, for instance, quickly became the largest producer of its kind in Europe (Lange 2015). The Norwegian policy turned out to be successful, as the country's industrial production in 1950 was 50% higher than its pre-1939 level. Its focus was on strengthening the heavy, power-intensive industries, which had previously produced electricity for their own consumption. But after 1945 the Social Democratic government decided that the state-owned power stations should begin to supply industry with more electricity. Consequently, heavy industry accounted for a growing share of Norway's gross energy consumption, reaching 46% in 1960. After 1970 this share declined as the country began to exploit its rich fossil fuel resources and to modernize homes based on increased energy consumption (Thue 1996).

The ERP was crucial to Norwegian reconstruction and growth policies, making it possible for Norway to import food, machinery for industrial production, and coal and oil. In a wider view, the ERP also helped open up the international economy, which Norway depended on to achieve growth beyond its domestic markets (Lange 2015; Pharo 2015).

The great acceleration came slightly later to Finland, due to its post-war situation and relation to the USSR. In 1948, the two countries signed the Agreement of Friendship, Cooperation, and Mutual Assistance, which precluded Finland's participation in the ERP. Instead, the post-war years until the mid-1950s became a prolonged period of reconstruction during which Finland had to pay heavy war reparations to the USSR, even while it remained in national debt from the war. Much of the Finnish industrial production sector became organized in trade deals, which included war deliveries and reparations. This proved beneficial to companies that produced goods that were interesting to the USSR, examples being Tampella (paper pulp machines, locomotives, weapons, and wood products) and Wärtsilä (marine and ship-building technology, such as diesel engines and iron mills).

After the period of war reparations ended and regulations were dropped, Finland entered a phase of rapid economic growth. Between 1950 and 1973, average annual growth was 4.2% (and thus higher than Sweden's rate). Be-

Cooking apparatuses around 1900
Both gas and electricity profoundly transformed everyday life, primarily in the kitchen, and until the 1960s there was keen competition between these two forms of energy. © Michelle Bridges / Alamy Stock Photo

tween 1948 and 1979, the annual average worker's income more than doubled. Finland's growth continued during the early 1980s, while other European countries were experiencing "staggering growth and structural crises" (Fellman 2008). From a labor perspective, Finland took a great leap from agrarian to service economy, with many agrarian workers transferring directly, bearing in mind that in 1960 about 40% of the population still lived in the countryside. As a result, when urbanization began there were not enough jobs in the towns and cities, and many Finns migrated to Sweden to find work opportunities between 1950 and 1980.

Iceland had a vulnerable and fluctuating economy for many years after the end of World War II. Prospects began to look better in the 1960s, but a high inflation rate continued to restrict economic growth (Björnsson 1967). The country's economic progress was a result of investments in modern sea fishery and the above-mentioned construction of power plants to utilize hydropower and geological energy.

One general consequence of the public sector growth trend and increasing employment was double-income families. This tendency of equalization was, to a great extent, related to the migration of rural, agrarian workers towards urban, industrial jobs, and also to the increasing participation of women in labor-market employment. Taking Sweden as an example, between 1950 and 1975 the public sector grew by 600,000 workers. At the same time, the number of women performing unpaid labor in Swedish homes decreased by 500,000 (Sjögren 2008). This meant that the average household with two adults earned substantially more in 1970 than in 1955 (Statistics Denmark 2014). Income increased more than inflation, and for ordinary people this was a golden opportunity to improve their living conditions – to make "the good life" better. One important first step was to leave the countryside, or move out of the city and into the suburbs.

This shift also enabled more people to access mass consumption. Many could afford a car, and often a holiday home as well.

Planning and housing

In the Nordic countries the 1950s was a decade of spatial planning. This was an important tool in optimizing the functioning of society, and as such it lay at the core of welfare state policy. The post-war boom saw an unprecedented development of housing across the Nordics, partly linked to the demographic changes outlined above. In many cases, residential construction was accompanied by welfare reforms that would ensure housing for families in different economic situations.

Many technocrats went to the US to study not only city planning, but also logistics and self-service developments like retailing and fueling stations, among other things. This was a part of "catching up" with the US after the stagnation caused by World War II. The wave of new urban planning inspired by American trends comprised several activities. One was the remaking of many city centers, where old buildings were torn down and replaced with modern shopping malls, pedestrian streets, and parking lots. As an extreme example, between 1960 and 1970 almost half of Sweden's old urban building stock was torn down to make way for new development (Lundin 2008).

In general, cities that had grown organically to accommodate pedestrians and bicycles were now refashioned to accommodate cars, and new housing was planned in line with the idea of separating cars, bicycles, and pedestrians, as well as separating work and home life (Braae 2022).

When World War II ended in 1945, the most pressing social problem was housing. The number of dwellings was insufficient, and part of the existing housing stock was ripe for redevelopment.

Against this background, the Danish parliament adopted an act supporting construction of new social housing and small single-family homes with publicly financed grants, obtainable on the condition of compliance with certain guidelines. The act was in force for 12 years, supporting the construction of 150,000 new dwellings. Even though this number was smaller than had originally been anticipated, the act had a huge impact, as it enabled many families to improve their living conditions by moving into either a small single-family home or an apartment in a social housing complex.

Much of the urban housing stock in Finland had been destroyed or lost during World War II, through bombings and the loss of territory. After the war an intense rebuilding period began, and from 1950 to 1975 the annual construction of residential units and homes rose from some 30,000 to about 77,000 (Meinander 2020).

Norway also lacked homes immediately after the war and aimed to construct as many new dwellings as possible at a fair rent or price. Like the other Nordic countries, the Norwegian state provided favorable loans for new homes, and from 1950 to 1995 more than two thirds of all new houses were financed by state loans. The number of new houses being built peaked in the 1970s.

As mentioned above, despite having been spared the destruction of housing during the war, Sweden still replaced much old housing with new, modern buildings. The iconic housing policy known as the "Million Program" was launched with the aim of building a million new homes, including whole new suburbs (Braae 2022).

The expanding financial headroom in the Nordics and the efforts to improve housing standards contributed to a great interest in architecture and interior design, including technological innovations such as new household appliances and improved heating systems, especially central heating – boosting the use of energy. As everyday life was energized, a new heating culture emerged, and life was electrified.

The "21-degree culture"

Central heating was initially based on coal burners, and later on oil furnaces or direct electricity, especially in Sweden and Norway. The use of energy for heating increased significantly and made a decisive contribution to energy consumption in the home. The average floor area per person increased, due both to larger dwellings and to a downward trend in the number of inhabitants per household. As of 2022, Danes generally had the most generous indoor living spaces, averaging 53.6 square meters (577 square feet) per person.

Central heating became widespread from the late 1940s. This technology replaced the traditional wood- or coal-burning stove, as well as gas and petroleum stoves, all of which emitted radiant heat, which made it impossible to heat rooms evenly. On top of that, the old fuel stoves emitted smells and potentially harmful fumes. By the late 1950s the construction of houses with traditionally fueled cooking stoves was coming to an end, and new kitchens of this type were mainly installed in rural areas.

Central heating improved everyday life by enabling more flexible room designs, since radiant heat restricted design options for indoor spaces. In addition, central heating helped to even out temperatures indoors, eliminating the traditional need for cold rooms or zones in the home, such as the entrance hall, corridors, and the "best room", which would only be used for Sunday dinners or entertaining guests. A more even, constant temperature in all rooms became common, creating what has been called the "21-degree culture", although 21° Celsius (70° Fahrenheit) must be regarded as a minimum, as many homes maintained higher average temperatures (Rüdiger 2022).

A higher standard of living does not necessarily lead to higher energy consumption if the energy is used more efficiently, for instance in connection with better insulation. However, until the oil crisis in 1973, low oil prices did not encourage insulation, at least not in Denmark. The welfare state also used more energy. The newly constructed non-profit social housing, public institutions, hospitals, kindergartens, and schools all needed light and heat and electricity for their spaces and electrical appliances, so the total heated space area increased in the 1960s (Rüdiger 2019).

Central heating could be based on either fossil fuels or electricity. In Denmark, central heating was based on coal-fired boilers in the 1950s, and this came with a downside. Coal or, more commonly, coke (a by-product of gas production) had to be shoveled into the boiler regularly, which was hard work. Coke was also dusty and smelly, and it took up a lot of space. A family with central heating would reap the rewards of its hard work when they were able to spend time together in a home that was heated to at least 21 degrees. In the late 1950s and into the 1960s, the interest in coal- or coke-based central heating declined, and oil burners, electricity, and district heating took over Danish space heating. An improved financial situation in most households enabled many to install an oil burner on their old boiler. For families moving to a new house in the suburbs, or into a new flat in an urban apartment blocks, the oil burner was the obvious choice.

The situation in Sweden was quite different. A surplus of electricity, after the expansion of both hydropower to the north and nuclear power, joined with the low prices proposed by Vattenfall to make electricity an important carrier of heating, in addition to oil boilers (Kaijser 1986;

Sjödin 2003). The bonus from this was better energy utilization, and thus cheaper heating.

Whether energy consumers chose a collective solution – district heating or electricity – or the individual oil boiler, two things were clear: The tedious work of distributing the heat into your various rooms disappeared; and the dependence on oil steadily grew. The smell, on the other hand, disappeared only for those who chose district heating or electricity as their preferred technology.

The installation of oil burners marched on as the technology won over suburb after suburb. The oil burner was the modern version of private, individual heating, and it replaced burners and household furnaces that used coke, coal, peat, or kerosene. During the 1960s, however, and most notably after the oil crisis of 1973-1974, collective solutions began to gain ground. The Million Program in Sweden included district heating as the preferred system, and in Denmark district heating was strongly subsidized from the 1960s. Finland, too, replaced the traditional use of timber and oil with district heating after 1970. In contrast, Norway has consistently focused on electric heating, while district heating only accounts for about 10% of space heating consumption. In Iceland, geothermal heating became more and more widespread from the early 1960s onwards.

And what about homeowners – how did private consumers benefit from the new heating culture? Danish advertisements for oil burners suggest an answer, showing what installations were sold, but they do not necessarily give a correct picture of people's wishes regarding the heating of their homes. Ads addressed to housewives declare that an oil burner is hygienic because it does not create dust, even while promoting health and well-being as a clean and comfortable heat source. Finally, it augments the flexibility of one's home décor. Ads that address the man of the house assure him that the oil burner provides

The modern electric kitchen
After World War II, the modern lifestyle materialized in functional kitchens with numerous electrical appliances. Today's focus on electrification for climate reasons has further emphasized the benefits of the electric kitchen.
© Derek Trask / Alamy Stock Photo

clean, economical heating and saves labor. Replace your coal boiler and you will free up space for a dining room or a game room! Families could now enjoy a well-heated house with all its creature comforts, including full bathtubs and long showers at a reasonable price. A new heating culture was established, improving physical comfort and well-being (Rüdiger 2021).

Electrification

Unlike the evolution of Nordic heating, the electrification of Nordic homes was generally similar to that in most of the Western world, because the new lifestyle of the 1950s and 1960s involved using more energy. This was very concrete and visible in modern homes, which were filled with appliances and installations that ran on energy, making energy dependency more pronounced.

Electricity also gained ground in public spaces, with streetlights, neon advertising, and electric transport options such as trams and trains. But electricity was expensive, so consumption only really began to increase in the late 1950s, when prosperity increased and oil and electricity became cheaper (Kander 2002). Politically, this development was not planned, but in the industrial policy mindset a better and more reliable energy supply with room for higher consumption was essential, and its foundation had to be an expanded electricity supply system.

Electrification was a gendered development, and one that was subject to social inequalities, as reflected in the fact that the kitchen was the first room in the home to be electrified. The inspiration from the American way of life was evident, and Sweden became the first of the five Nordic countries to pick up on this inspiration and translate it into the national tradition. After electric lighting had become the norm (Kaijser 1986), a large number of electrical appliances found their way into the kitchen and utility room in particular, and also into the living room. Refrigerators, freezers, washing machines, electric mixers, and a growing host of other consumer durables and gadgets became a part of modern living from the 1950s onwards. In their free time, families could also enjoy televisions, radios, gramophones, and cars, or purchase one of the increasingly popular charter holidays by plane to countries with a warmer, sunnier climate than any of the Nordics can offer.

The electrification of homes was an important aspect of post-war modernization in the Western world, and it took place in the wake of the high economic growth of the late 1950s and 1960s, accompanied by low energy prices. Furthermore, this modernization was characterized by changes in the energy mix, with oil as the increasingly dominant fuel in Denmark and Finland, whereas oil only partly replaced coal and hydropower or geothermal power in the other three Nordics. Most importantly, electricity was perceived as better suited to the modern lifestyle than firewood, coal gas, and other legacy fuels. Power was not only cleaner and safer, it could also be used for a greater number of time-saving appliances and entertainment devices, such as radio and television. The access to cheap, abundant oil allowed a far more diverse use of energy than before.

Even though the five countries' timelines differed, the prevailing modernist idea was that a rational, efficient kitchen had electrical appliances. The development of new, versatile plastics and microelectronics led the way in the development of a whole new world of household electronics. The "fridge" made it easier to take care of easily perishable purchases from the supermarket, keeping meat, vegetables, milk, beer, wine, and leftovers fresh regardless of weather and room temperature. Together with the stove and sink, the refrigerator was one of the three basic necessities of every self-respecting kitchen. At-home freezing also became popular in the Nordics. Cold storage on a cooperative basis had been popular in rural communities for a couple of decades, but the trend was overtaken when freezers became a durable household commodity, as each family got its own.

Roughly the same thing happened with the washing machine, which, being an expensive appliance, was often shared by several neighbors. From the late 1950s it became more common for newly built houses to be equipped with their own washing machine, or at least plugs and outlets for one. The large-scale washing of former times – for instance, a laundry day once a month – would soon be replaced by far more frequent washing of lighter textiles. In spite of the Nordic climate, clotheslines did not disappear, although tumble dryers became more and more popular.

Besides the refrigerator and the washing machine, a number of other appliances found their way into the kitchen: the electric stove, dishwasher, food processor, and microwave oven, to mention but a few. All of them ran on electricity. As a result electricity consumption increased three- to fivefold from 1950 to 1970, with Denmark and Finland as the least electricity-hungry among the Nordic countries.

Transport

In global terms the Nordic capital cities are small, although each one is still the most populous in its nation. But after World War II, they all realized that urban planning was necessary as one of several tools to manage housing shortages and – from a more farsighted perspective – to address growth, urbanization, and other demographic changes.

Both Stockholm and Copenhagen published general plans drawing on the British "garden city" concept introduced by Ebenezer Howard. These plans regulated urban growth so that it would take place in satellite towns, radiating from the central city along corridors or "fingers", as they were called in the Danish plan (Braae 2022; Maudsley 2022). The suburbs were a mix of apartment blocks and areas reserved for single-family dwellings, connected to the city by trains and highways (Hansen & Jespersen 2009). But planning had its flip side. The plans were based on an expectation that people could and would find work near their homes, but instead they began commuting. Meanwhile, no connections had been planned between the fingers, which all pointed to and from Copenhagen or Stockholm city center, without any new "webbing" infrastructure in between. To go from one finger to another, one had to either go through the city center by public transport or take the car. More and more people preferred the latter alternative, resulting in heavier traffic.

The modernization of the housing sector, outlined above, had the unintended consequence of increasing transportation needs. Mopeds, motorbikes, and cars grew more popular, partly because of the greater distances between home and work. This prompted the building of more highways and freeways, and also an expansion of public transport systems.

In 1953 the first Swedish freeway was opened, and three years later a Danish freeway followed. Subsequently the number of cars per thousand inhabitants increased tenfold in all the Nordic countries (Statistics Denmark 1964; The Danish Ministry of Taxation 2021). All in all, private car travel grew rapidly, freight traffic largely shifted from rail to road, agricultural operations replaced horses with tractors, and air travel became more common.

From 1948 freight transport by truck exploded, and continued to grow at a rapid pace. This affected transport by horse-drawn trucks, railways, and domestic sea transport. From the 1960s the constantly and rapidly growing volumes of global trade were increasingly transported in "shipping containers", a trend that benefited both truck and rail transport. Air freight transport also increased in the 1960s, although airplanes were mainly used for passenger transport. The rising number of air travelers reflected the business community's need to move faster, as well as the popularity of charter tourism.

Scandinavian Airline System, or SAS – then jointly owned by the three Scandinavian countries – was the first airline to introduce a "tourist class" in 1952, making flights affordable to those who were not business travelers. Still, only a small minority of the population had ever flown before the rise of charter tourism. Such trips were initially organized by train or bus, later by airplane, and they became popular in the 1960s as an affordable way of enjoying sunny beaches and warmer climates.

The desire to own a motorized vehicle on vulcanized rubber tires was inextricably linked to the emergence and expansion of the suburbs. Driving was a necessary part of the daily transport triangle between home, daycare or school, and work. Commuting surged, and a growing proportion of the traffic took the form of gasoline-powered vehicles. This was not regarded as a problem at the time. Oil and gasoline were cheap, and no one talked about air pollution. The development of the welfare state was well under way, helped along by the trusty internal combustion engine.

The growth of transportation was highly dependent on the use of oil and oil derivatives. The environmental impact of this soon became obvious. Air pollution, also in the shape of smog, was a companion of individualized transport, but because transportation was – and is – intimately related to other aspects such as economic planning, trade, and tourism, it has been difficult for nations to reduce its negative impacts without adversely affecting other sectors.

The decades of "great acceleration" transformed Nordic societies and encompassed virtually all aspects of living, including the development of welfare states and infrastructures, daily life, consumption, and travel. In material terms these changes rested on a dual basis of fossil fuels and large-scale electricity production (initially based on hydropower expansion in Sápmi), and in terms of ideas they grew from the interlinked ideals of economic growth and abundant energy access. The transformation improved the quality of life for Nordic populations, but it also led to lifestyles that have later proven to be unsustainable, both socially and environmentally. Many of the global challenges societies face today are rooted in this acceleration and in persistent path dependencies observable in infrastructures and behaviors that originated during that period.

Chapter 5.
Nordic energy in a wider world

The Nordic countries are part of a regional and global energy system, and their integration intensified after World War II. As relatively small economies, they are dependent on exports and imports, and on the relationship between the two. For example, the traditionally important industries of both Finland and Sweden, such as steel manufacturing and pulp processing, are energy intensive; they are also key export industries for both countries. Access to cheap energy is therefore crucial if such industries are to compete on a global market with lower prices. However, the details of these trade dependencies and how they relate to energy and resource trade look different for the five countries.

Looking at energy source imports included in the 2015 official statistics of the International Energy Agency, or IEA (namely coal, oil, natural gas, and electricity), Norway had net exports of 581%, while the other Nordic countries had net imports of 45% (Finland), 25% (Sweden), 12% (Iceland), and 2% (Denmark) of their net energy use (Worldbank.org). As for their development over time, more recent data show that energy imports to Sweden and

Finland have slowly declined since 2004, while Icelandic imports have been declining since 2018.

Norway is the clear outlier here as the largest Nordic energy exporter by far, thanks to its export of oil, gas, and some electricity. Oil and gas represented almost 60% of Norway's total exports in 2021. While oil was easily the larger export commodity during the 1980s and 1990s, from the 2000s onwards gas exports have increased, and in 2021 gas made up well over 50% of Norway's export of fossil fuels. Norway is a relatively small player on the global oil market, but it ranks third among global gas exporters, outranked only by Russia and Qatar (norskpetroleum.no). In 2022 Norway increased production and surpassed Russia as the main provider of gas to Europe. The other Nordic countries are currently net importers of crude oil and natural gas, although Finland, Norway, Sweden, and Denmark are net exporters of refined oil products. Denmark has an interesting trajectory, having been a net energy exporter from 1993 to 2018, then turning into a net importer (except in the case of natural gas) with imports rising slightly, primarily due to the depletion of its North Sea oil fields (IEA 2022). This trajectory is likely to continue, based on the Danish parliament's adoption in December 2020 of a cutoff date of 2050 for all oil and gas extraction in their part of the North Sea, and the cancellation of all future licensing rounds to external operators (Danish Ministry of Climate, Energy and Utilities).

The cross-border exchange of electricity among the Nordic countries has a long history, starting with the exchange cooperation Nordel. Since the integration of the common EU market for electricity in 2009, all Nordic countries except Iceland have imported and exported electricity through an integrated grid. Currently, Norway and Sweden are net exporters of electricity while Finland and Denmark (the latter just barely) are net importers (Swedish Energy Agency 2022; Stattnett 2022; Statistics Finland

2022; Danish Energy Agency 2022). We will return to this development in the next chapter on energy markets.

As noted above, the IEA numbers include coal, oil (both crude and refined), natural gas, and electricity. However, other imported resources also contribute to the total energy use of most countries. Taking Sweden as an example, if we include the import of uranium and biofuels, over 60% of the Swedish energy supply is based on imported raw materials, despite Sweden having its own national sources of biofuels, wood, and uranium, as well as hydropower (see Kaijser & Högselius 2019). Some nuclear fuel is produced in Sweden by a Westinghouse factory, intended for both internal use and export, but the uranium for fuel production is imported. In Finland, nuclear power makes up almost 35% of electricity production (2019), and the nuclear fuel is imported from Russia, Sweden, and Spain (Statistics Finland 2022). Both Sweden and Finland source their uranium on the world market, mostly from Kazakhstan, Australia, and Canada. Biodiesel, bioethanol, and biogas, as well as raw materials for producing bioenergy (mainly wood, rapeseed oil, palm oil, and animal fat), are imported goods (albeit of differing importance) for all Nordic countries (Statistics Norway 2022; ET 2022: 09; Swedish Energy Agency 2022; Danish Energy Agency 2022). Thus, the Nordics' overall dependence on imported energy resources is greater than can be seen in most statistics. This hidden import dependency has many facets, one of which is that certain fuels are generally envisioned in the public debate as national energy sources or carriers, and therefore their import aspect is rarely mentioned. This has been the case for nuclear power in Sweden and also for forestry resources in Finland and Sweden (Åberg & Fjaestad 2020).

Despite this, the degree of import dependency has decreased in all five Nordic countries since the 1970s. Up until the first oil crisis in 1973–1974, energy imports had been increasing, in correlation with the processes of the "great acceleration" discussed in the preceding chapter. By 1973, in the Nordic countries imported fossil fuels accounted for 52-98% of each country's energy use, with Denmark and Sweden as the most import-dependent countries and Iceland and Norway at the opposite end of the dependency scale (Worldbank.org).

Although the problem of foreign energy dependency had been acknowledged earlier, the oil price shock in 1973, and the second oil crisis in 1979, led to a more radical rethinking of the import-reliant energy systems that existed in many countries. This led to forceful interventions by governments, and tangible changes in citizens' daily lives. The crisis also revealed the heightened but often "invisible" role that energy systems played. State interventions in the Nordic countries came in the form of encouraging citizens to save electricity, combined with investments in new energy sources and heightened efficiency in buildings and industrial operations. In Denmark, which was severely hit by the crisis, an energy savings commission was created, and massive energy conservation measures were imposed on citizens: gas rationing, turning down the heat, and promoting car-free Sundays. In terms of energy system changes, oil was largely replaced by coal, leading to sustained high levels of carbon emissions, which in turn created problems when energy policy gradually turned into climate policy with emissions-reduction goals from the 1980s onwards. Nevertheless, because coal was also to some extent imported, it was not until the Danish natural gas grid was fully rolled out in the early 1980s that Danish energy imports began decreasing in earnest (Rüdiger 2019; worldbank.org).

In Sweden the state also launched energy conservation campaigns, encouraging citizens and small businesses to save energy to allow industries to stay up and running, thereby saving jobs too. The state led by way of

Krafla geothermal power plant, northern Iceland
Insulated high-pressure steam pipelines running from one of Krafla's 33 boreholes to its turbines. This geothermal power plant was a pioneering endeavor when it started up in 1974. Today, Krafla has an installed capacity of 60 MW.
© Frantisek Staud / Alamy Stock Photo

example, saving electricity in their own public agencies while teaming up with municipal, state, and private energy producers, private oil distributors, and a wide variety of organized non-governmental energy-use stakeholders to decrease energy consumption. The aim was to avoid harsh rationing, and the Swedish strategy proved to be successful (Vedung & Hansén 2019). In the long term, state and industry acted by continuing to develop nuclear power, invest in research programs on energy efficiency, and collaborate with heavy industries (especially in paper and pulp) to replace oil with biofuels (Bergquist & Söderholm 2016).

In Iceland energy imports had already begun decreasing from 1940, but in the 1970s the country developed geothermal power and hydropower at a pace that slashed the use of heating oil from 50% of household heating consumption in 1973 to just 5% in 1985 (National Energy Authority of Iceland, NEA; Melsted 2020). Finland, although affected by higher market prices and stagflation problems following the oil crisis, was still to some extent protected against major trade balance deficits – a common occurrence in other countries – due to its import relationship with the USSR (Fellman 2008).

Specifically in terms of Nordic energy imports, aside from countries' internal attempts to deal with their energy shortages and high prices, new patterns of import diversification arose. During this period the oil and gas deposits found on the continental shelf in the North Sea started producing, as we will discuss in greater depth in the next chapter. Norway's development of its oil and natural gas fields enabled a shift on a regional scale, creating an opportunity for the Nordic countries to diversify their oil imports and secure their supply closer to home, instead of trading with the OPEC countries as they had done previously. For countries like Sweden and Iceland this shift led to a dramatic turn away from oil producers in the Middle East to more regional trade with Norway. Denmark could exploit its own North Sea oil and gas fields, and natural gas especially became a game changer in the Danish energy system. Even so, as noted, Denmark was only a net exporter of oil and gas for a short period. (Rüdiger 2011; IEA).

Finland, on the other hand, held a particular role in the Nordic geopolitical space in terms of regional relations. After the war, Finland signed an Agreement of Friendship, Cooperation, and Mutual Assistance with the USSR, as mentioned above. This agreement recognized Finland's right to stay out of the geopolitical power struggle, allowing the Finns to adopt a policy of neutrality during the Cold War while agreeing to terms of mutual assistance in case an attack was launched on Finland, or on the USSR through Finland. Conversely, this also meant that Finland did not participate in the US-funded Marshall Plan and, in the longer term, did not join NATO or the Warsaw Pact. A main symbol of the friendship agreement was increased Soviet-Finnish trade. Oil was a major Soviet export commodity, and as early as 1948 the USSR captured a substantial share of the Finnish oil market, to the detriment of

Western oil imports. During the 1950s over 90% of Finnish oil imports came from the East Bloc (Jensen-Eriksen 2007). In 1967, Finland was the first Western country to set up a permanent commission for economic cooperation with the Soviet Union.

In the late 1960s Finland had a deficit on its trade balance with the USSR and several large trade contracts were concluded to remedy this, including one for natural gas (Åberg 2013). While this development worried other Western actors – who feared not only the loss of their own market shares, but also that the situation could become a "weaponization of energy" that would hold Finland hostage – it is important to note that Finnish actors did not passively accept the Soviet oil hegemony. Instead, they acted with creativity to maximize Soviet imports, which were seen as the best alternative to promote Finnish national security and welfare (Matala 2022).

Since Soviet trade was based on a bilateral trade-clearing system, a symbiotic relationship developed in which some Finnish manufacturing became dependent on exporting to the USSR. Importing oil and energy sources was one way of evening out the trade balance between the two sides. The fact that Finnish oil imports were organized within this trade-clearing system meant that when prices rose during the oil crises, Finnish export opportunities to the USSR grew accordingly. Thus, Finnish oil imports became inextricably linked to the textile and metal industries, in particular, up until the early 1990s. One consequence of this was that employment in Finland stayed high (Fellman 2008; Matala 2022). Although Russian oil imports took a downturn around the time of the fall of the USSR due to supply and availability issues, they later recovered, and in 2021 Russia was the single largest provider of oil products and natural gas to Finland (Statistics Finland 2022). However, as we saw in Chapter 2, this situation changed abruptly in 2022.

Statoil rig in the Norwegian part of the North Sea
Norway began producing oil and natural gas in the Ekofisk field in 1971, and Statoil was founded the following year. In 2021, oil and gas accounted for 60% of Norway's total exports. © Neil lee Sharp / Alamy Stock Photo

From a longer historical perspective, the import and export patterns in the Nordic countries have developed quite differently. Often, imports are a consequence of a certain resource being scarce in a given country, for example due to geographical circumstances. In most Nordic countries except Norway, as we have seen, this is true of fossil fuels and also of products like palm oil, which is used in biofuels, and uranium.

However, over time imports have often been a consequence of economic reasoning. For example, in the 1950s and 1960s Sweden was considered to have the largest uranium deposits in Europe, yet today the country imports all its uranium. One reason for this is that Swedish uranium would cost too much to extract. In the late 1950s, calculations showed that extracting uranium in Sweden would be 70% more expensive than importing it from the US (Åberg & Fjaestad 2020). Similarly, in the interwar period Sweden and other countries were already experimenting with creating national fuels for cars, the goal being to avoid importing oil. In comparison, however, the locally produced alternatives always turned out to be more expensive (Ekerholm 2012).

Another common situation affecting imports is that countries with national extraction of a certain resource may become highly dependent on importing that same resource due to a high level of consumption, which in the long run necessitates imports. We have already mentioned Finnish and Swedish import dependence on wood products. Denmark offers another case in point, as the Danish state decided to invest in natural gas infrastructure based on gas finds in the North Sea. This infrastructure promoted the use of natural gas, and now consumption exceeds the national resources available (DEA).

The types of cross-border import and export flows in the Nordic countries are also connected to infrastructure investment and logistics. For example, in the early stages of the energy trade, oil and coal could easily travel between the Nordic countries through the available transport infrastructures, allowing for easy import with very few regulations. In some instances, regulation came later, if at all. As an example, Sweden suggested a tax on coal imports at the end of the nineteenth century. This was deemed impossible, however, since it was seen as too hard on users who depended on coal for heating (Kaiser & Högselius 2019). This policy on coal, which had flowed freely before that time, led to highly coal-dependent Swedish customers.

The coal infrastructure in the Nordic countries is very different from the region's natural gas infrastructure. While the European natural gas networks cover almost all countries in Europe, leading into the North Sea, North Africa, the Middle East, and Russia, there are only two gas pipelines that cross a Nordic border: one from Russia into Finland, and the Danish-Swedish connection. The newly inaugurated Baltic Pipe offshore pipeline (2022) also transports gas from Norway to Poland, with Denmark as a transit country – benefiting Danish gas consumers if needed.[12] Considering the pipelines that have historically been

12. The Nord Stream pipelines pass through the Baltic Sea across Danish territorial water and the Swedish and Finnish exclusive economic zones, but they do not connect to a gas grid in any Nordic country

constructed across the former Iron Curtain and the Mediterranean region it seems somewhat ironic that friendly neighbors as culturally close as Denmark, Finland, Norway, and Sweden have not been able to establish internal connections of this sort. In many other sub-regions of Europe gas sources have been developed slowly, first catering to one country, then to its neighbors, but despite the presence of natural gas in the Nordic region, natural gas links between the four closest Nordic neighbors are conspicuously lacking. One reason for this is that the Swedish grid, which would geographically be placed in the middle of a hypothetical Nordic gas grid, remained limited. This was primarily because it was difficult for natural gas to enter the Swedish energy market, and because of the country's energy-related climate debate, which intensified in the 1980s (Åberg 2013).

All Nordic countries are currently and have historically been interwoven in a web of global energy flows, often to an even greater extent that one might reasonably expect. The ways in which these energy flows have been regulated and organized has also changed over time, and this is the topic of our next chapter. Early on, fossil fuels were brought to the Nordics through international oil majors, mainly from the Middle East, but energy policies and energy systems were perceived as national issues. The development of North Sea extraction and EU-initiated liberalization furthered a regionalization process that would cover most of Europe with gas and electricity grids. Simultaneously, the climate crisis and its aim of achieving a massive green transition have become international issues that are changing trade patterns (for instance in the biomass trade) while simultaneously questioning the extractivist trade regimes of the past.

Chapter 6.

Infrastructures and markets

The public sector has played a crucial role in planning and building critical infrastructure over the past century. The most notable infrastructure systems carry water, energy, sewerage, railways, and telecommunications.

The development of Europe's infrastructures took off in the early nineteenth century, with energy as one of the later examples. In the Nordic region, from the end of the 1800s local authorities played an important role in not only the production of gas and electricity but also the building of local infrastructures, for example street lighting and tramways. Around the time of World War I, the public sector became the most important player in grid-based supply systems, while the extraction and trade of coal and oil remained in private hands. Local networks were also linked to much wider systems through trade in these two types of fossil fuel (Högselius et al. 2016).

In the interwar period, energy infrastructures were expanded, but they were also hampered by a lack of reach and by limited demand, which utility companies tried to remedy through advertising and renting electrical appliances to customers at low fees. In some cases local systems were supplemented with cross-border links. In 1915, for instance, a connection was established between Sweden and Denmark to bring Swedish hydropower to Copenhagen and its environs, but this link was only of local importance (Wistoft et al. 1992).

The transition from direct to alternating current, which began in the early twentieth century, helped to centralize electricity production. The centralization of power systems was one main feature in the development after World War II promoted by the European Recovery Plan (ERP, also known as the Marshall Plan, as noted earlier). Up until that time, developments had predominantly been national, with cross-border connections playing only a subordinate role. In Sweden and Norway hydropower was regionalized in the interwar period, also aided by the state (Thue 1996; Högselius & Kaijser 2007).

The centralization of Nordic power production proceeded rapidly after 1950, driven by collaboration between electricity companies and state planning bodies that wished to achieve rational, stable production and expand their grids to cover entire communities, and indeed their societies at large. The utility companies became larger and fewer in number.

It was not until the 1960s that cross-border links began to be seen in the region. In 1963, a Nordic power collaboration called Nordel was established among the largest producers in each of the four mainland countries, with Iceland not participating for obvious geographical reasons. Nordel coordinated the expansion of high-voltage connections between the four countries, also tabling recommendations for *samkøring*, literally "co-running" or "pooling operations", in an effort to expand cooperation among power plants and ensure better utilization of the available resources (Lagendijk & van der Vleuten 2013; Högselius & Kaijser 2007).[13]

13.
In 2009, Nordel's tasks were transferred to ENTSO-E

14.
HVDC is an efficient method for transmitting large amounts of electricity

15.
The linking of the two legacy "power regions" in Denmark was only achieved in 1998, as part of the integration of the continental European network

As one of the first high-voltage direct-current (HVDC) connections[14] in the world, the Konti-Skan connection between Denmark and Sweden was established in 1965.[15] Since then the four Nordic countries on the European mainland have been interconnected by a number of cables and also linked to the neighboring countries of Germany and Poland, the three Baltic countries, and Russia (Michelsen 2013), thereby making the Nordic electricity system part of the continental European network.

The European energy market changed profoundly when a huge gas field at Slochteren in the Netherlands was discovered in 1959. Before that time, the household gas supply was organized in local networks mainly based on coal gas and, to a much lesser degree, on natural gas. Neighboring countries began to import Dutch gas, and in 1968 the USSR began exporting gas from even larger fields in Siberia, first to Austria and later, from 1974, to Finland (Högselius 2013; Högselius et al. 2016). With the discovery of oil and gas fields in the North Sea the growing interest in natural gas also came to the Scandinavian countries. Norway began producing natural gas in 1977, and Denmark followed suit in 1984. The following year Sweden was connected to the Danish gas grid, but even today it is striking not only how little the Nordic countries have been connected to the European gas network, but also how little they are connected with each other, as noted in the previous chapter.

As gas production was regionalized and Europe was integrated through an extensive network of pipelines, storage facilities for natural gas came to play an important role for the security of supply in the European gas system. There are only three large-scale natural gas storage facilities in the Nordics: two in Denmark, and one in Sweden.

State-owned energy companies

In the construction of national energy systems and the establishment of energy markets, state-owned companies have played an important role in the Nordics, in keeping with the region's tradition of public bodies influencing the supply of essential services and amenities.

The public sector has therefore exerted considerable influence on energy systems throughout the last hundred years. This situation is embedded in the theory that technical conditions can make a network operate better, more efficiently, or more economically with one company in control than with two or more players vying for dominance. In principle it is not profitable to have multiple gas and power grids; the issue is not whether the owner is a private or public company. However, in the Nordic countries a perception crystallized early on that if energy systems were to be efficient, all-encompassing, and cheap, then energy would be a task for the public sector. Some might describe this as a welfare state approach, but supplying energy to citizens also gave local authorities an opportunity to expand their revenue base beyond tax collection, as explained earlier.

The state-owned companies entered the energy field at very different times. Sweden was first, with the establishment of Vattenfall in 1909, while the rest of the Nordic countries followed rather later, after World War II.

Sweden: Vattenfall

Using the Swedish word for "waterfall" as its name, the company Vattenfall was founded in 1909 by the Swedish state to exploit large-scale hydropower opportunities and provide easy access to cheap electricity – something the authorities did not believe private companies would guarantee. In some cases factories set up hydropower stations of their own, and Vattenfall primarily produced

Power distribution at Hällefors, Sweden
Cross-border links between the Nordic power networks were developed from the 1960s onwards. In 1963, the Nordel collaboration was set up to coordinate connections and exchange power between countries, as and when deemed effective.
© Bo Jansson / Alamy Stock Photo

power for industrial operations, including the railways, while supplying only a relatively small number of households. Especially during World War I and after World War II, rural electrification was also an important task for Vattenfall. The company's first power station began operating in 1910, and it quickly became the dominant electricity producer, with a market share of around 30% in the 1930s. This later grew to around 50% in the 1980s (Högselius 2009; Lundberg 2009).

Like other state-owned companies, Vattenfall served the interests of the nation and the public and complied with political mandates and requirements. On the other hand, ownership issues aside, the company also shared interests with other players in the electricity market. Basically, the state – as the owner of such a company – had the right to decide how far such interests could be pursued. However, it is important to emphasize that although Vattenfall was state-owned, there was no attempt to nationalize it, so it had a certain flexibility to maneuver in the market (Lundberg 2009; Högselius 2009).

The policy of centralizing Sweden's energy supply was expressed not only in Vattenfall's dominant position, but also in the fact that in 1937 the country's many local networks were linked by a transmission network that ran from south to north. The southern regions were developed in the early 1930s, after which the authorities began to focus on the resources in the northern regions of Sweden and Sapmí.

From the mid-1950s Vattenfall became a central player in the development of nuclear power, which – like oil and combined heat and power (CHP) – became an alternative to hydropower. Diversification and more cooperation among power plants made the system more resilient, and the security of supply was strengthened to counteract natural hydropower fluctuations (Högselius & Kaijser 2007).

As shown in Figure 2.3, Swedish electricity consumption grew rapidly until the mid-1980s, giving electricity producers excellent growth opportunities in a constantly expanding domestic market.

By the 1960s nearly all of Sweden's households had been electrified. Vattenfall continued to gain ground in the domestic market by successfully investing in electric heating, and by expanding CHP in the early 1970s. Nuclear power was expanded in the same period, and in 1969 Vattenfall began constructing its first nuclear power station with light-water reactors (Vattenfall.com). However, opposition to nuclear power was increasing, and after a referendum in 1980 the Swedish parliament adopted a decision that aimed to phase it out by 2010 at the latest.

As the EU pursued its plans to create an internal market, the nature of the EU and Nordic energy markets shifted. In theory the era of state monopolies was a thing of the past, but in practice, due both to natural monopolies in the way the transmission grids were organized and to differences in the various companies' market reach, Nordic energy customers can still see elements of monopolies today. Nevertheless, in the 1980s and early 1990s the lack of market competition in the region was increasingly seen as an obstacle to developing an efficient and cost-efficient sector that would benefit businesses and private consumers alike. Sweden was not yet a member of the EU, but similar ideas gained a foothold there, which became firmer against the backdrop of Sweden's economic crisis.

The first step Sweden took was to transform Vattenfall into a limited company. No longer an energy-policy instrument, it was run according to the logics of competition and profitability. The next step was a more general deregulation, allowing electricity consumers to freely choose their power supplier. In 1996, as the third step, Sweden was linked to the Norwegian spot market, which had been formed in 1993 to operate on the deregulated Norwegian market, and which was now called Nord Pool ASA. This gave Vattenfall access to the Norwegian market, and this link, combined with deregulation, enabled it to expand beyond Sweden's borders (Högselius & Kaijser 2007; Lundberg 2009).

The company's subsequent expansion in Europe was rapid, taking the form of either acquisitions or mergers with Dutch, German, Polish, Danish, Finnish, and British companies or elements in the energy system, such as power plants or wind farms. In the early 2000s Vattenfall had already become the third-largest electricity producer in Germany. One aspect of this expansion was that Vattenfall's share of the fossil fuel market increased, but renewables also gained prominence and became an important part of the company's portfolio. This particularly applied to offshore wind farms and, to a lesser extent, solar power. In 2016, 75% of the company's investments were in onshore and offshore wind farms (Vattenfall.com).

Norway: From Statoil to Equinor

Both Norway and Denmark came late to the oil industry. This factor, combined with the difficult extraction conditions in the North Sea, explains much about why, from the 1970s to the mid-1990s, the companies operating in this area were at the forefront of offshore technology development (Ryggvik 2015).

The first concession round took place in 1965, and the first oil discovered in the Norwegian fields, more precisely in the Ekofisk field, was found in 1969 by non-Norwegian operators. They also started up production, but the discovery made Norwegian politicians realize that Norway's participation was imperative. In 1972 the Norwegian parliament decided to establish the state-owned limited company Statoil and an administrative body called the Norwegian Petroleum Directorate, or NPD (Ryggvik 2015).

State-owned companies were not a new thing in Norway. In the decades after World War II several commissions and inquiries had discussed the subject. When the "Norwegian oil adventure" began with large discoveries in 1969–1970, there was a clear public demand that extraction ought to serve national purposes. On the other hand, there was no consensus on how a state-owned oil company ought to be organized, or on what tasks it ought to undertake. The relationship between state and company was therefore a subject of contention, interestingly with the Labor Party advocating the least possible interference from parliament, while the Conservatives wanted more state control.

The result sought to balance private and public ownership, and in practice the company enjoyed considerable independence. Statoil did not initially engage in downstream activities, but it later came to participate in the whole scope of activities, from oil exploration to selling oil-based products to customers (Hanisch & Nerheim 1992).

The NPD, set up as a government counterpart to Statoil, was tasked with handling the political, administrative, and financial control of Statoil, and also with building a solid base of geological and technological knowledge about natural resources offshore. Norway therefore established a triangular model with Statoil as the state-owned commercial oil company, NPD as the regulatory body, and the Ministry of Industry as the politically responsible government body that also handled licenses and set tax levels (Hanisch & Nerheim 1992; Lerøen 2019).

By dividing the Norwegian continental shelf into independent blocks and granting a license for each block, Statoil was quickly able to become involved in exploration and production, even though at the outset Norway had neither the necessary skills nor any competitive edge over foreign operators.

Statoil's first crucial task was to influence the path of the pipelines running to land from the Ekofisk field. Its efforts met with only partial success. The next vital task in the North Sea was to gain control of the promising Brent field, where Statoil ended up with 50% ownership (Ryggvik 2015). Statoil became an operator for the first time in 1981, in the Gullfaks field.

In the early phase of Statoil's history, beginning in 1974 the company partnered with the partly state-owned company Norsk Hydro and the private company Saga Petroleum – a partnership that not only reflected the sheer magnitude of Norway's opportunities in the North Sea, but also illustrated the traditionally close relationships that were possible between private and public players.

In the early 1980s, Statoil became a fully vertically integrated oil company after entering downstream activities, acquiring existing gas stations and expanding them into a network of service stations. In Denmark and Sweden, for example, Statoil purchased gas stations from Esso in 1985, doing likewise in Ireland with purchases from BP in 1992. In the 1990s, Statoil also built up a sales network in Eastern Europe (Ryggvik 2015).

The political disagreements about Statoil did not disappear, however, and Norway's center-right government of the early 1980s clipped the company's wings. A body was founded in 1984 that was designed to keep the petroleum industry in check: the State's Direct Financial Interest (SDFI). This body transferred part of Statoil's licenses to the Norwegian state, which thus came to manage significantly more oil reserves than Statoil, and which ensured that the state received a direct share of petroleum revenues. The reform also benefited Statoil, however, giving it the freedom to expand internationally (Lerøen 2019; Ryggvik 2015).

From the mid-1980s onwards, and especially after oil prices plummeted in 1986, Norwegian oil policy became more market-based and less protectionist. As a result, more oil production was placed in Norwegian hands, a development which – in light of Norway's close relationship with the EU's Internal Market – must be seen as an attempt to gain the benefits of the internal market without being a member of the EU.

The next step in deregulation was the partial privatization of Statoil in 2001, which listed the company on the stock exchange and reduced the state's share to 81.7% – a share further reduced to 70.9% in 2005. At the same time the Norwegian state established a new state-owned company, Petoro, to handle SDFI interests. In this context a fifth of the state's assets were sold, mainly to Statoil. The privatization measures were followed by a merger of Statoil with Norsk Hydro's oil and gas division in 2007 and a further reduction of the state's share to 67%. And because these two companies had already acquired a share of Saga Petroleum in 1999, the Norwegian three-company model ended with their merging into one large entity in 2007 under the Statoil name (Lerøen 2019; Ryggvik 2015).

In 2015, Statoil created a division for renewables. To signal its shift towards a more diverse portfolio it set out a new strategy in 2017 and changed its name to Equinor in 2018 (equinor.com).

In terms of volume, Norwegian oil production peaked in 2001 at 3.4 million barrels per day. In 2013 this number had dropped to 1.3 million barrels, ending up around 2 million barrels per day in 2021. In contrast, gas production has steadily increased, with gas exports mainly going to Germany and Italy.[16] The war between Russia and Ukraine and the EU's decision to rapidly reduce Russian gas imports, as well as the inauguration of the Baltic Pipe, will presumably mean a growing demand for Norwegian gas in the years ahead.

16.
The figures cover total production, not only production in the North Sea

Denmark: From DONG to Orsted

In 1972, Danish Oil and Natural Gas (DONG) was founded as a fully state-owned company. Its mission was to negotiate natural gas purchases with foreign operators to fill Denmark's planned natural gas grid, as one of the strategies to reduce the country's dependence on oil. DONG's efforts at negotiation failed, but the first national Danish energy plan (1976) still appointed the company to build up a natural gas supply in Denmark to diversify the energy options. The gas fed into this network would come from the Danish part of the North Sea, where Maersk Oil and Gas and the Danish Underground Consortium (DUC) would produce it and sell it to DONG.

Both the transmission network, which DONG handled, and the distribution network, which regional companies handled, were completed in 1984. In the meantime the Social Democratic government had adopted new regulations for oil and gas exploration, which meant that DONG became a "carried partner"[17] in all new licenses.

17.
This means the company has a share in a license without making any investments

This status would ensure that the Danish state got a share of the profits from the natural gas extraction while building its knowledge of the processes involved. When the EU decided to deregulate the energy sector, however, this state-market model was no longer viable, which challenged DONG on two counts. First, Danish energy companies broadly believed that size really mattered for energy companies wishing to compete on the future European energy market. Second, the former state monopolies were expected to lose customers on their domestic markets to players on the spot market (Voldsgaard & Rüdiger 2021; Rüdiger 2011).

Bolstering itself for the race ahead, DONG chose to expand its portfolio and become an energy company that in addition to its previous tasks also produced and sold electricity. It thus became a company with interlinked activities, along similar lines as major European players such as the German company E.On.

The most obvious way for DONG to achieve its goal was to acquire municipal electricity companies from Danish local authorities which, due to deregulation, wanted to sell off their activities in the energy sector – since in the new situation municipalities were allowed neither to profit from nor to suffer a loss on such activities.[18] In 2006, after a long and dramatic process, DONG merged with five other electricity companies, covering Denmark in its entirety and taking the new name of DONG Energy (Rüdiger 2011).

There were widely differing competence areas, operational areas, and corporate cultures in this new, comprehensive company, which called for a new, unifying strategy. The question was whether DONG Energy ought to continue along the fossil fuel track, or whether it ought to invest in renewable energy. And an even more fundamental question was: Should it continue as a Danish company or merge into a European company?

Keskiputous hydroelectric power plant on the Tammerkoski channel, Tampere, Finland
The first two state-owned energy operators in the Nordics – Vattenfall, founded in Sweden in 1909, and Imatran Voima, founded in Finland in 1932 – were hydropower companies, indicating the central role hydropower played in both countries. ©Jani-Markus Häsä / Alamy Stock Photo

18. This is referred to as the "principle of cost-recovery"

19.
The panel recommended that global emissions had to be reduced by 50% by 2050. The following year, the EU adopted its visionary 20-20-20 targets

The wider context of these decisions included a Danish political shift towards an increasingly more positive attitude to "green transition" thinking. Copenhagen was to host the COP15 process in 2009, and both the IPCC's fourth report and the Stern Report were published in 2007.[19] The gateway to a greener path was swinging open, but large investments were tied up in the production of fossil fuel energy, and parts of the DONG Energy organization were skeptical about renewables.

The company's new strategy, formulated in 2008, implied a turnaround. The strategy was referred to as "85-15" to signal DONG Energy's aim to reverse the relationship between fossil and renewable energy in the company's portfolio, going from focusing on fossil energy to the majority of the company's activities being linked to renewable energy by 2040. Although DONG Energy was a minor player in Europe, the company's ground-breaking decision would make it a global leader in offshore wind. Assuming we include biomass as a renewable energy source, the company achieved its 85–15 target in 2019.

DONG Energy already had experience in building and scaling up offshore wind farms. The company itself defined three conditions for success: a growing market for offshore wind, strong partners, and a financing model that could reduce capital costs by making wind turbine production more industrially sound and scalable, and more rational (Voldsgaard & Rüdiger 2021).

The Danish company's activities rested on public procurement, for instance in the UK, where DONG Energy, usually in collaboration with Siemens Wind Power, built several offshore wind farms. The financing model largely lived up to expectations, although the company ran into a financial crisis in 2012–2013, resulting in partial privatization, new management, and stronger focus on sustainable electricity production. To reflect the shift, in 2017 the company changed its name to Orsted, the anglicized surname of the Danish scientist H.C. Ørsted, who discovered that electric current can produce magnetism.

In recent years the company's portfolio has been expanded further to include Power-to-X[20] and green-energy islands located, for instance, in the North Sea (Orsted.com).

Finland: From Neste to Fortum

Fortum Oy is the main state-owned energy company in Finland. It was established in 1998 as a merger of two government-owned companies: Imatran Voima ("Imatra's power") and Neste Oy. The first of these legacy companies dates back to 1932 and was founded to construct and operate the hydropower plant at the Imatra Rapids in southeastern Finland. Following this, it operated several other hydropower and coal-based power stations (fortum.com).

20. "Power-to-X" is a collective term for conversion technologies that turn electricity into carbon-neutral synthetic fuels, for instance liquid hydrogen, or into chemicals

Neste Oy (roughly translated, "liquid fuel limited"), on the other hand, was an oil refining company founded in 1948. Before World War II, Finland imported all of its oil and petroleum products, a situation that caused severe shortages during the war. The new company's first task, however, was to construct a storage facility for fuel oil and lubricants; it was not authorized to build a refinery until 1954. Refinery operations began in 1957-1958. A second refinery followed ten years later, and around the same time Neste entered the field of petrochemical production. When Finland signed a contract with the USSR in 1971 concerning natural gas imports destined for the Finnish industrial sector, Neste installed the grid and organized the gas distribution.

In the early 1970s Neste already had an international market presence through a number of partnerships, including interests in an oil field in Oman and transactions in the US market. It further diversified its portfolio in the 1990s, moving into the plastics industry and becoming responsible for the pipeline that transported natural gas from Russia to Finland.

After the merger in 1998 Fortum divested the oil and petrochemicals businesses, and in 2005 it exited its last vestiges of oil exploration and production, including upstream activities in Russian oil and gas fields. These activities were transferred to Neste Oil. Additionally, the Commission of the European Union requested that Fortum reduce its stake in the gas grid connecting Finland and Russia, and the company complied.

Instead, the company has focused more on renewables and nuclear power. Its main activities are operating over 150 Fortum-owned or co-owned hydropower stations in Finland and Sweden, and running nuclear power stations in both countries. Fortum also sells electricity and electricity products and runs CHP plants in Norway, Poland, and Russia. Part of its power generation uses fossil fuels, but especially in Finland the production is based on renewables. Fortum is targeting carbon neutrality by 2035 for its European production, and by 2050 for its activities in other parts of the world.

Iceland: Landsvirkjun

The Icelandic energy market has traditionally been dominated by publicly owned companies, in particular the state-owned company Landsvirkjun, but with large municipal authorities as other important actors.

Iceland's national power company, Landsvirkjun, was founded in 1965 by the state and the City of Reykjavík to generate and distribute hydropower to southern and western Iceland. In 1983 one of the northern municipalities became a part-owner of the company.

In 2003 the Icelandic parliament decided to transform Landsvirkjun, in line with EU deregulation. The company was unbundled and the transmission grid transferred to a subsidiary. Since then the trend has been moving towards a more diverse ownership structure (Allemand et al. 2016). Today, Landsvirkjun covers approximately 75% of Iceland's electricity production.

Deregulation and new markets

In 1986 the EU launched an ambitious plan to improve competition in the Internal Market, defining energy production as a sector of particular interest. Part of its rationale was the sector's tendency to be organized in "natural monopolies" with extensive public interference, aimed at providing businesses and citizens with a reliable supply of cheap energy. The EU's liberalization – or deregulation – of the energy sector was defined as a massive reduction in public interference and the scaling back of natural monopoly elements to a minimum, in order to introduce competition in the energy sector. An excellent example of such a monopoly would be owning and operating a transmission or distribution grid. The initiative was intended to expose the energy sector to competition, not to achieve a deregulated sector, and consequently the outcome – rather than *deregulation* – was a sort of *re*-regulation or a new regulatory regime. Although privatization was never a part of the exercise, the process changed the nature of energy companies from natural monopolies to companies subject to competition, which therefore focused on the bottom line. From an EU Commission perspective, the important thing was to create energy systems with all aspects of the market exposed to competition, except the transmission grids. Whether energy companies were private or public was of no interest, as long as they complied with the rules laid down by the Commission, such as unbundling.

The resulting process was not without flaws, however. Many member states were cautious about exposing all parts of their energy sector to competition. This was predictable, since public monopolies formed the backbone of the energy system in several member states. Moreover, widespread subsidization (at least those measures not in accordance with the market) was an obstruction to competition. A third challenge was the lack of transborder transmission networks, which limited cross-border energy trading (Buchan & Keay 2015).

Even before the Common Energy Market was implemented, competition was introduced to the British and Nordic electricity markets. Nordic deregulation began in Norway in 1993, addressing the monopolistic structures and the regionalized power sector by creating an exchange or a "trading floor" for electricity. Two years later, when the Swedish electricity sector joined, this forum turned into a spot market with day-to-day trading under the name of Nord Pool ASA. In 1998 the Finnish electricity sector followed suit, as did Denmark in 2000. Consequently, the energy companies in all four of these countries had to comply with the EU directives and adjust to the spot market.

Compared to the preferential markets before the rise of deregulation – or liberalization – the new market conditions unleashed new company behaviors. First of all, consolidation and internationalization were two strategies employed by all important energy companies. Furthermore, there has been a strong tendency towards a more narrowly focused portfolio, including the divestment of transmission pipelines and grids to non-profit public companies. In addition, combined with climate targets, all Nordic state-owned companies now have renewables as a vital part of their activities. Finally, deregulation helped to improve the situation for up-and-coming producers of renewables and to increase their space and opportunities on the energy market.

The history of Nordic state-owned companies is similar to that of other European energy companies. They played a vital role in constructing the energy systems at a national and European level, and they contributed to the rise of smoothly functioning welfare states. The Europeanization of the sector meant that national energy regimes were transformed, and most were exposed to competition with the aim of achieving more efficient systems and affordable energy for consumers. This process has been neither easy nor straightforward, and its success has been debated. Nevertheless, it has impacted the regulatory regimes of these energy systems, thus setting a new framework in place for how to organize and implement a possible system transition in the future.

Chapter 7.

Nuclear power

Although the fear of nuclear weapons grew with the escalating arms race and the test detonations of the Cold War era, back in the 1950s the notional possibility of promoting the "peaceful use of the atom" had met with great enthusiasm. After President Dwight D. Eisenhower's launch of the Atoms for Peace program in 1955, nuclear power was expected to be a major element in meeting the world's growing need for energy and a potential replacement for coal and oil. On the scientific side, researchers strove to find out how nuclear power could best be utilized, which type of reactor was most efficient, and how nuclear waste could be handled safely.

Other groups expressed their anxiety about nuclear technology, often referring to the link between atomic weapons and nuclear power, and to the fear that power plant systems might fail. The main specters were reactor meltdowns and the radiation they would release, as well as the long-term storage of nuclear waste.

Historically, the five Nordic countries have had very different attitudes to nuclear power. Finland and Sweden both use nuclear power today, and the decision to introduce it must be seen in the light of the rising demands for electricity in the face of limited hydropower capacity and a lack of fossil fuels in both these countries (nordics.info). In Sweden's case, national access to uranium also played a key role. While Finland intends to continue to use nuclear power, Sweden decided to phase out its plants after a referendum in 1980. This decision may be reversed, however, as there are new trends in Swedish policies and public opinion. Norway and Denmark did in fact decide to introduce nuclear power too, but both countries postponed their decision in 1979. Iceland has not found nuclear power relevant as an energy form. Finally, it is noteworthy that Sweden and Denmark have both seen significant popular movements against nuclear power that have been strong enough to influence the political agenda.

In all four countries where nuclear power was seen as a relevant option, the struggle between advocates and opponents lasted several decades. Agendas have shifted, going from enthusiasm over the "atomic age" in the 1950s to a peak of resistance in the 1970s and 1980s. Today, many in the Nordics are reassessing the potential that nuclear power may hold, in the wake of the global climate crisis and the Russian–Ukrainian war. Geopolitical aspects also continue to play a role, as Finland imported not only natural gas but also uranium from Russia.

Barsebäck nuclear power plant, Sweden
Barsebäck, inaugurated in 1975, has been called "the world's most inappropriately placed nuclear power plant" due to its location on the west coast of Sweden, not far north of Malmö – and in plain sight of the most densely populated area in Denmark: the capital region, which lies due east across the Öresund strait. © UtCon Collection / Alamy Stock Photo

Nuclear power as part of the future

As early as November 1945, the Swedish government set up its Atomic Committee (AC) to investigate the options for using nuclear power for civil and military purposes, and the possibility of using Sweden's large deposits of low-grade uranium to become self-sufficient in nuclear fuel. The company AB Atomenergi was formed to handle these tasks, with the Swedish state as the largest shareholder, supplemented by private capital. The Atoms for Peace program and Sweden's ensuing collaboration with the US, along with the formation of the International

Atomic Energy Agency (IAEA) in 1957, led to the country scrapping its nuclear weapons programs to focus on the civil use of nuclear technology (Grimstedt 1995).

Initially the program was developed to use Swedish uranium in heavy-water reactors, thus keeping the entire nuclear fuel cycle in Sweden. This would have been crucial, had the ultimate goal been to develop nuclear weapons. It proved to be an extremely expensive technology, however, and when others around the world began to develop commercial reactors and the price of nuclear technology fell, Swedish power companies instead turned to the US, where cheaper light-water reactors were being built. Although this made Sweden dependent on enriched uranium from other countries, such reactors were installed in the first plants put into commercial use in Sweden.

Non-government-owned utilities also had interests in nuclear power, and this led to the formation of the

Atomic Power Consortium, which investigated other options than those the AC did, including the various types of reactors. Many negotiations followed, and in 1965 the consortium signed an agreement with the Swedish electrical engineering company ASEA for construction of the Oskarshamn nuclear power plant, with boiling-water reactors and a power output of 400 MW (Grimstedt 1995). The Oskarshamn plant was commissioned in 1971.

The idea of self-sufficiency was abandoned, but not until the mid-1960s. The possibility of buying American enriched uranium brought private actors into the field, so the production of nuclear power became a mix of public and private enterprise. On the other hand, the increased risk of import dependence encouraged the government to set up a special body to deal with this risk, and with the problem of enrichment (Åberg & Fjaestad 2020).

Sweden's subsequent build-out of nuclear power was rapid. Between 1971 and 1985 the country built four nuclear power plants with a total of 12 reactors and a capacity of more than 10,000 MW. The future seemed promising, and the power utilities invested to expand electric heating by means of new tariffs, even as they developed the distribution networks to handle higher effects.

In the 1950s and 1960s hydropower expansion came under attack from a growing movement uniting Sámi associations, nature conservationists, and tourist organizations. This led to a government decision to spare the four remaining rivers in northern Sweden from hydropower development. Nuclear power was seen as the way to cover an anticipated rise in energy consumption. But during the 1970s opposition to nuclear power surfaced and grew in many countries. Sweden was no exception. Nuclear power became a highly contentious political issue, affecting governments and culminating with the Three Mile Island meltdown at a nuclear facility in the eastern US in 1979. Against this backdrop a Swedish referendum was held in 1980, which resulted in a decision to phase out nuclear power before 2010 while considering the need to supply electricity. Thus, the 12 planned or already operational nuclear reactors would be built and used before being decommissioned. Nevertheless, in 2020 eight reactors were still active, supplying about 30% of the electricity produced in Sweden. A small part of this 30% is exported to Denmark. In other words, the intended phase-out has not taken place yet, nor is it clear whether it will. While some of Sweden's political parties have long been divided or opposed to the phase-out, others have changed their position over time. Public opinion has also slowly shifted – it is now more in favor of nuclear power in light of the climate crisis and the energy supply crisis. While opinions and regulations are currently changing, however, there are still no concrete plans to build more nuclear power plants in Sweden.

In Finland the interest in nuclear power intensified after the first Geneva conference in 1955. Two years later a national atomic energy commission was set up, and in the years that followed it oversaw the construction of an experimental reactor for research use only (Jåfs 2009). As in many other countries, however, the state's ownership in the energy sector was a contested issue.

Hydropower expansion had reached its limits in the 1960s, a situation which had already been foreseen by the Finnish state and the industrial sector. Industrial actors regarded nuclear technology as an interesting option, but state actors were more skeptical. There had previously been conflicts over the ownership of power production in relation to developing hydropower, an area where state-owned companies and private companies competed.

While the Finnish state did not start up a large-scale nuclear program, investments were made in nuclear research to prepare the country for future introduction of nuclear power. In the 1960s, both state-owned and privately owned companies investigated options for purchasing full-scale nuclear power plants, but it was state-owned Imatran Voima (IVO) that was first off the mark in putting such a plan into practice. Nevertheless, the tense Cold War situation would prove to be an issue for the Finnish state. IVO first invited bids from Western companies, but it soon became clear that they could not avoid purchasing from the USSR. After intense negotiations an arrangement was made under which certain safety features would be purchased from Western countries while the reactor itself was purchased from the USSR. This hybrid deal worked out so well that IVO ordered a second power plant on similar terms.

Meanwhile, the forestry industry and its associates wanted to retain control of their own energy supply, and in 1969 sixteen large Finnish industrial and energy companies founded their own nuclear power company, called TVO, and began the process of buying nuclear reactors. At the time these companies, taken together, consumed 40% of Finland's electricity supply, but they also produced a third of that supply. They were therefore important actors on the Finnish energy market, but they were also in serious conflict with the government, where strong voices were suggesting a fully state-owned energy sector. In the end TVO had to make a deal under which their nuclear power plant would be a public-private partnership, but they managed to avoid buying a reactor from the USSR. Instead, they purchased two reactors from the Swedish company ASEA-Atom.

The 1980s saw an attempt to expand nuclear power in Finland, supported by the industrial sector, as timber had become more expensive and paper processing no longer produced as many by-products that could be used for energy purposes. At this time the relationship between TVO and the state had improved, and the two sides began to collaborate towards building a new nuclear reactor. But the anti-nuclear movement had gained ground, and the accident at the Chernobyl nuclear power plant in Ukraine, which led to fallout all the way up to the Nordic countries in 1986, proved to be the last nail in the coffin for that project (Jensen-Eriksen 2020).

Popular opposition to nuclear power was met by a broad industrial coalition that insisted nuclear power ought to be expanded, and the climate debate of the 1990s gave them another argument, emphasizing that nuclear power does not cause carbon emissions once a plant is up and running. Against this background the Finnish parliament decided in 2002 that a fifth reactor was to be built. This was the first time since Chernobyl that a Western country had planned to construct a new nuclear power plant. The project ran into problems and has been postponed several times, but commercial production is expected to begin in 2023.[21]

In Denmark and Norway the idea of using nuclear energy for peaceful purposes also met with widespread support initially, and both countries entered the international research collaboration on nuclear energy. As early as 1951 the Norwegians commissioned their experimental reactor, JEEP-1, followed seven years later by another, the Halden reactor. Two more Norwegian reactors were commissioned in the 1960s. This work was carried out by a public body called the Institute for Energy Engineering. In 1969 the Norwegian parliament decided that nuclear power was to be part of national energy planning, due to uncertainties about how much hydropower could be developed. Nuclear power would thus increase the diversity of the country's energy system.

Similarly, Denmark set up its Atomic Energy Commission in 1955, with the Copenhagen physicist Niels Bohr as chairman. Three years later the Danes inaugurated their nuclear research establishment at Risø, where three

---

21. In 2010 and 2014 the Finnish government made decisions-in-principle on two additional projects

experimental reactors were installed (Petersen 1996; Nielsen 1998).

"Nuclear Power? No Thanks"

As mentioned earlier, in the 1950s there was much enthusiasm about the potential of nuclear technology in Denmark and Norway, and both countries were involved in efforts to develop safe, efficient nuclear power plants. Despite this, neither moved beyond the research phase to construct any commercially operational plants. There were several reasons for this. The first was the technology's association with nuclear weapons, which played a key role during the Cold War, causing fear among the public (Sylvest 2022). Secondly, during the 1970s a growing movement questioned the safety of nuclear power plants, and in certain circles this questioning attitude was supported by a criticism of the notion of limitless economic growth. A majority in the populations of these countries was also opposed to the unresolved aspects of nuclear power technology, particularly the issue of radioactive waste, which made such undertakings appear unnecessarily risky. The Three Mile Island accident heightened the levels of concern.

The confrontations around nuclear power technology were strongest in Denmark, perhaps because of its neutral history and more detached association with NATO, but the relationship between the state and the electricity companies also played a role. The transition of nuclear power activities from research institutions to production companies was a conflict-ridden process, a fact that probably contributed to delaying their transition into power production.

The electricity companies in western Denmark cooperated in a body called ELSAM, which managed the exchanging of energy between plants. ELSAM and parts of the industrial sector feared that the introduction of nu-

"Nuclear Power? No Thanks" Danish activist Anne Lund created this logo, widely known as the Smiling Sun, in 1975. Shown here as a street mural in Vestergade, Aarhus, the Smiling Sun became a Nordic and later global symbol for opposition to nuclear power. © mauritius images GmbH / Alamy Stock Photo

clear power in Denmark would mean nationalization of the electricity sector, and they were also dissatisfied with Risø's collaborating with the Swedish semi-state-owned AB Atomenergi to develop a heavy-water reactor. The electricity companies wanted to import a turnkey light-water plant. They further doubted that nuclear power, given the limited Danish market, would be able to compete with the cheap, abundant oil of that period. Only around 1970 did ELSAM believe the time was ripe to introduce nuclear power, and in response to the oil crisis in 1973 it proposed that Denmark begin constructing a nuclear power plant, which the government immediately supported (Petersen 1996).

However, as the discussions and conflicts unfolded, a new mood of opposition emerged. In 1972, a report entitled *Limits to Growth* was published by the Club of Rome,[22]

22.
The Club of Rome is a non-profit organization founded in 1968 by industrialists and intellectuals. Their first report, *Limits to Growth*, provided scenarios for the future of the global environment

and nuclear power as part of the growth discourse became a main topic for the peace and environmental movements emerging in several countries. In Denmark, concern swelled when the designated location of Denmark's first nuclear power plant was made public: Gyllingnæs, located on the coastline in the central part of the Jutland peninsula. These groups of concerned and critical citizens formed new organizations, the most powerful of which was the Organization for Information on Nuclear Power, known simply as the OOA. The "no nukes" groups got a huge boost when the nuclear power plant Barsebäck, located on Sweden's southwestern coastline, was commissioned in 1975. As this plant is located only about 20 kilometers from central Copenhagen, it was an apt symbol around which to rally the anti-nuclear movement (Rasmussen 1997; Kaijser & Meyer 2018).

Skepticism and public calls for more information on the risks of nuclear power increasingly turned into opposition, and when the Three Mile Island incident occurred immediately before a major energy policy debate in the Danish parliament, nuclear power was put on hold. Although the opposition groups lost momentum after that, the OOA managed to sustain anti-nuclear-power sentiments by using Barsebäck to emphasize the risks. In 1985 the parliament decided that nuclear power would no longer be an option in Danish energy planning.

In view of these developments, the Barsebäck power plant has been called the world's most inappropriately located nuclear power plant (Kaijser & Meyer 2018). Its location specifically meant that, at the same time as Barsebäck was helping to expand the Swedish electricity grid, it was also undermining Sweden's and especially Denmark's nuclear power strategy.

A similar development took place in Norway, where Three Mile Island also put a stop to the country's ideas of introducing nuclear power, and following the growing opposition in the population, nuclear power was rejected as an option in 1986 (snl.no).

Nuclear power revisited

Nuclear power continues to play a role in the Nordic countries today, but only Finland has taken any new initiatives. The prevailing attitude in the other countries has been that nuclear power must be phased out.

The debate refuses to die, however. Some groups, especially in Finland and Sweden, staunchly maintain that nuclear power is a relevant contribution to the energy supply. One argument is that the use of thorium, an element found in large deposits in Norway, has contributed to a more positive attitude towards nuclear power. Many years of experimentation with fusion energy point in the same direction.

The political scene shows a clear division, with supporters mainly found among the political right, while center-left parties generally oppose nuclear power. Overall, a majority in the populations of the three Scandinavian countries has been opposed to nuclear power since the 1980s. However, in view of how difficult it will be to meet climate targets, and due to the energy crisis caused by Russia's invasion of Ukraine, the mood seems to have shifted, with a small majority in favor of nuclear power. Its status as a carbon-neutral energy source has sparked a new interest in seeing nuclear power as part of the solution to the climate crisis. In parallel, the war in Ukraine has emphasized the need to reduce and eventually eliminate dependence on Russian gas altogether, without increasing consumption of the other fossil fuels. Nuclear power is being revived as an energy option that fits this double bill while also being promoted as a stabilizing factor in an energy system based on wind and solar energy. Time will tell whether these arguments are able to outweigh the considerable concerns about nuclear power as an energy form.

At one time, all the Nordic countries except Iceland were interested in, or even enthusiastic about, the potential peaceful uses of nuclear power as a means to secure a safe, stable, and unlimited energy supply, paving the way for a prosperous future. As we have seen, things turned out differently. It is striking that from the late 1960s onwards, public opinion had a strong impact on countries' decisions about whether to use nuclear power. The movements opposing nuclear power have had a long-lasting impact, clearly stating that the alternative to nuclear power was renewables – solar and wind power – even before these technologies were realistic alternatives. In the final analysis, describing an alternative probably contributed to the positive overall attitude in the Nordics towards what we now know as the green transition.

Chapter 8.
Conclusions

The world is currently facing the momentous challenge of accomplishing rapid energy system transitions to achieve multiple goals to promote social and environmental sustainability. Countries have very different starting points for this transition, but in practice, for most the shift entails moving away from (imported) fossil fuels and increasing the share of renewable energy in their energy systems. There are many drivers for this development, including climate change, health concerns, an enduring energy access gap, and energy security. These are all drivers that have also previously affected the Nordic energy systems in different ways. In recent times, at least in Europe, the shift has also been prompted by a willingness to decrease dependence on Russian energy, particularly natural gas, in the wake of Russia's invasion of Ukraine. The Nordic countries are no exception to this trend. They all have ambitious goals concerning the proportion of renewable energy in their energy systems. However, there are many hurdles to overcome, and the preconditions for such a transition differ among countries and regions. The Nordic countries are no exception in this respect either.

In general, all renewable energy – which in this context includes wind power, solar power (thermal, photovoltaic, and concentrated), hydropower, tidal power, geothermal energy, and biofuels – is more or less dependent on geographical circumstances. As we have seen in the preceding chapters, however, these energy forms are also part of a global market and therefore in some respects less bound by geography. A quick look at the share of renewables in total energy production in the various Nordic countries shows Iceland (86.87%) and Norway (71.56%) in the lead; Sweden (50.92%) in third place; and Denmark (39.25%) and Finland (34.61%) a close fourth and fifth (Our World in Data). Taking a closer look at these numbers, we see that Iceland and Norway excel in electricity generation, both boasting 100% renewable electricity production, due mainly to their large capacity for hydropower. Denmark and Sweden have 68% and 62% of renewables in their electricity production, respectively, while Finland reached over 50% of renewables in electricity in 2020 (National Energy Authority, Iceland; Statistics Norway; Energimyndigheten 2020; ens.dk). However, if we instead look at *non-fossil fuel* electricity, both Sweden and Finland score higher (Sweden reaching 100%) due to their use of nuclear power. In general, space heating is also provided by renewables to a great extent in all countries. It is fair to say that the Nordic countries have come far in terms of the shares of renewables in their energy mixes, and also in reducing their carbon emissions in a global context, at least if we consider territorial emissions.

On the other hand, as we have seen, post-war developments – fueled by cheap electricity, easy access to oil, and state-supported infrastructure development, among other things – resulted in energy-hungry societies. Norway and Iceland are still remarkably high in global comparisons of per capita consumption, and Sweden, Finland, and Denmark also rank near the top of the list. The example of

Iceland shows us that although the country's energy system shifted from the predominance of coal and oil over to hydropower and geothermal power, the change is only relative. In actual numbers, Iceland's consumption of fossil fuels increased continuously, from 4.7 PJ in 1940 to 19.7 PJ in 1980, and 48.8 PJ in 2018 (Melsted 2020). In addition, if we look at numbers for CO_2 emissions, adjusted to include emissions imported via trade, both Denmark and Sweden are among the countries with the highest non-territorial emissions in the world (Our World in Data). This makes it clear that although all the Nordic countries have transitioned parts of their energy systems, their transport sectors and adjustment for trade show that the Nordic societies, including those that do not produce oil, are still intrinsically dependent on fossil fuel consumption and, through a global market, they are a part of what has recently been dubbed a "global petroculture" (Millkrantz et al. 2022).

One of the most challenging sectors in the transition to renewables is transport. Despite this, Finland and Sweden were the only two EU countries that exceeded the 10% target for 2020 set by the renewable energy directive (2009/28/EC), with their share of transport sector renewables at 15% and 30%, respectively, due to their high level of biofuel use. Norway also boasts a high level of renewables in transports (20% in 2018), as a forerunner in electric vehicles. In 2022, almost 80% of private cars sold in Norway were EVs (Ranta et al. 2020; Transportochlogistik.se). The fact that transport still seems more resistant to change has multiple explanations. A major factor lies in the Western world's culture of consumption and its ideal of the accelerating lifestyle outlined in Chapter 4. Individual consumer behavior, including consumption of travel and of goods that increase emissions from international trade and transportation, are deeply intertwined with the everyday lives of people in the Nordic countries. This entanglement involves key ideas of identity, status, personal economy, cultural practices, media, and myth, drawing, for example, on a history of coinciding trajectories of the rise of the car society, as well as the changes in consumption that cars brought about (see, for instance, Cowan 1983; Lundin 2008; Egan Sjölander et al. 2014).

Another challenge is the issue of land use, which has to do with the geographical siting of new large-scale energy infrastructure. This includes local and national opposition to chosen sites, balancing different kinds of land use and environmental harm, and debates over resource distribution. Historically, hydropower expansion has been contested at different times in all the Nordic countries except Denmark (which does not have hydropower). The earliest hydropower opposition in Sweden came from farmers who were contesting small-scale exploitation of waters previously used for various other purposes. In the 1960s and 1970s environmentalists opposed large-scale dam projects based on ecological concerns, leading to a moratorium on further exploitation of Swedish rivers (Jacobson 1996; Haikola & Anshelm 2016). Hydropower development has also met with opposition in Norway, and the "Alta conflict" over hydropower development in the Alta and Kautokeino rivers became a pivotal event that gathered many different actors against hydropower development in the 1970s. This proved to be a turning point in the relationship between the Norwegian state and the Sámi population inhabiting the country's northern regions (Engen et al. 2023). As mentioned in Chapter 2, in Sweden, Norway, and Finland, large hydropower dams that supply populated centers in the south have historically been constructed in Sápmi. These projects have obstructed traditional land use and reindeer herding, and also damaged the natural environment. In addition, the compensation for damaged land and livelihoods has been lacking or insufficient (Össbo 2023; Össbo & Lantto 2011; Österin & Raitio 2020; Engen et al.

Middelgrunden offshore wind farm in the Øresund strait
This wind farm is located near two major cities, Copenhagen and Malmö. They are linked by Öresundsbron (the Øresund Bridge) between Denmark and Sweden, seen here in the background. Wind power is one of the most rapidly growing energy sources in the Nordic region today. © Stephen Dorey Creative / Alamy Stock Photo

2023; Mustonen et al. 2010). Such developments were a key element in the colonization of Sápmi. In the light of this history, indigenous advocacy groups have labeled the current interests of national governments in developing more hydropower and erecting large-scale wind farms as "green colonialism", pointing out the risk of perpetuating colonial power structures (thebarentobserver.com).

One core issue is how to distribute the proceeds of exploiting natural resources. Norway has developed a tax system that compensates municipalities for resource extraction taking place in the north, including compensation for hydropower (Energy Facts Norway). There are ongoing discussions regarding the inclusion of wind farms in this taxation policy, and regarding the consequences this would have for wind farm development. Despite wind being one of the fastest-growing energy infrastructures in the Nordics, both land-based and offshore wind farm expansion have met with resistance over the past 20 years in all Nordic countries, and this trend seems to continue. Denmark has historically been considered a forerunner in the field, thanks to its processes for community participation in planning wind farm activities, which have been seen to increase acceptance for the construction of wind farms. However, the regulatory approaches in Denmark have recently been criticized too. Today there is considerable opposition to wind farms, and several municipalities are now rejecting proposals for further land-based wind power development within their borders (Claussen et al. 2021). Alongside these debates, there is an ongoing discussion about how much land, crops, and forests ought to be used to obtain biofuels. As an example, a study of the sectoral roadmaps to reach a carbon-neutral Finland in 2035 shows that, taken together, they contain a total of biomass use that massively oversteps available forest biomass in Finland (Majava et al. 2022). The sustainability of using biomass as a fuel instead of as a carbon sink and for protecting biodiversity is also disputed by many researchers (Toivanen 2021). This illustrates the increasing complexity of pursuing the green transition agenda and expanding the sustainable energy supply.

In short, the further expansion of renewables comes with several social, technological, and economic challenges. Additionally, the current energy crisis has highlighted social challenges, especially in times when price rises may widen class divides in financial terms. Governments are caught between the demand for a more ambitious climate policy and more urgent calls to support businesses and low-income households by lowering taxes on fuel or subsidizing disadvantaged citizens' electricity bills. This issue has been further complicated by the ongoing integration in the EU common market, and by Russia's invasion of Ukraine. In view of these challenges, and combined with the projected increase in electricity demands, Finland and Sweden (both members of the EU) are arguing the case for keeping nuclear power as part of the EU "green taxonomy", to make sure it is branded and perceived at least as sustainable, if not as renewable.

A related issue is the fact that the very term "transition", and the concept of historical energy transitions, is now being questioned by researchers who point out that, looking at long-term global trends, it is very rare to see new energy sources actually replacing older resources (York et al. 2019; on the difficulty of fossil fuel replacement in particular, see Vinichenko et al. 2021). Indeed, they suggest that we use the concept of "energy addition" until such time as renewables properly replace fossil fuels in the long term. Globally the use of fossil fuels has continued to increase, except for a short and exceptional lull during the COVID-19 pandemic, after which it quickly rebounded. From a Nordic perspective the use of fossil fuel in Sweden and Norway went down in 2021, but only by 0.57% and 0.3%, respectively. Iceland remained at the same level as the preceding year, and Denmark and Finland increased their consumption, albeit slightly (by 3.62% and 0.19%, respectively). Furthermore, the annual change in fossil fuel use shows a very slow decline since the 1980s, bordering on stagnation, a pace that does not match the rise in the use of renewables (Our World in Data). As pointed out in Chapter 2, a high share of renewables in a country's energy mix does not automatically translate into a smaller carbon footprint or lower energy use per capita. One coming challenge is therefore how to make sure that changes in energy systems really feed into a genuine transition, rather than just being an addition.

Taken together, the challenges of fundamentally changing our energy systems and consumption patterns are monumental, even in the Nordic countries, which have come a relatively long way in terms of territorial emissions. This means that certain changes to the energy systems must happen quickly, but also in a socially sustainable way. How can we transition away from Russian gas quickly, but without getting stuck in new unsustainable patterns? How do we make sure the transition does not increase gaps between population segments in terms of finances and energy access and that its negative externalities are evenly distributed? Solutions to these issues are currently being debated in all the Nordic countries. Often such debates are polarized between, on the one side, those who believe technical solutions will allow us to continue our "business as usual" lifestyle and, on the other side, those who believe our behaviors and activities must be fundamentally changed, as Earth's resources cannot sustain a high-energy lifestyle for the global population. Pursuing such debates leads us into issues such as political governance versus market solutions; individual action versus structural change; and the responsibilities of richer nations towards less affluent nations. The preferred solutions tend to be mirrored in the political landscape and tie into fundamental political and ideological philosophies. This makes it difficult to find common ground and reach agreements.

Meanwhile, these pressing problems must be solved quickly and effectively, and not just in the Nordic region. While the Nordic countries generally have a relatively high proportion of renewables, they have still not fully crossed the line between "transition" and "addition", as outlined above. One reason for this is that a full-fledged transition is more complex and diverse than an energy system transformation. The breakthrough of fossil fuels and the great acceleration after World War II show that the indispensable pieces of this puzzle include not only technological solutions, but also political, economic, and cultural decisions, combined with new behaviors and daily practices. And the puzzle must be solved if we are to comply with climate targets and ultimately find a sustainable way of living.

Suggestions for further reading

Melsted, O. (2020). *Icelandic Energy Regimes Fossil Fuels, Renewables, and the Making of a Low-carbon Energy Balance, 1940-1980*. Dissertation, University of Innsbruck.

Matala, S. (2022) National Security, Security of Supply. Finlandisation as a Diplomatic Practice and the Finnish Energy Dependency on the Soviet Union, 1948-1992. *The International History Review* Vol. 45 No. 3, 551-571. https://doi.org/10.1080/07075332.2022.2155212

Ryggvik, H. (2015). A Short History of the Norwegian Oil Industry: From Protected National Champions to Internationally Competitive Multinationals. *Business History Review, 89*(1), 3-41. https://doi.org/10.1017/S0007680515000045

Sperling, K. & Rüdiger, M. (2020). Liberalization of the Danish energy sector – an era of turnabouts. In Arler, F. et.al. (2020) *Ethics in Danish Energy Policy*. Routledge.

Össbo, Å. (2023) Hydropower histories and narrative injustice: state-owned energy companies' narratives of hydropower expansion in Sápmi. *Water History*. https://doi.org/10.1007/s12685-023-00328-z

References

Allemand, R. et al. (2016). Local Government and the Energy Sector: A Comparison of France, Iceland and the United Kingdom. In H. Wollmann et al., *Public and Social Services in Europe. From Public and Municipal to Private Sector Provision*. Palgrave Macmillan. https://doi.org/10.1057/978-1-137-57499-2

Bergquist, A. K. & Söderholm, K. (2016). Sustainable energy transition: the case of the Swedish pulp and paper industry 1973-1990. *Energy Efficiency, 9*, 1179-1192. https://doi.org/10.1007/s12053-015-9416-5

Björnsson, O. (1967). Economic Development in Iceland since World War II. *Weltwirtschaftliches Archiv, 98*, 218-240.

Braae, E. (2022). *Urban Planning in the Nordic World*. Aarhus University Press and the University of Wisconsin Press.

Buchan, D. & Keay, M. (2015). *Europe's Long Energy Journey – towards an Energy Union?* Oxford University Press.

Clausen, T. L. et al. (2021). The good process or the great illusion? A spatial perspective on public participation in Danish municipal wind turbine planning. *Journal of Environmental Policy & Planning, 23*(6), 732-751. https://doi.org/10.1080/1523908X.2021.1910017

Cowan, R. S. (1983). *More Work for Mother: The Ironies of Household Technology from the Open Hearth to the Microwave*. Basic Books.

Danish Energy Agency, DEA. ens.dk/en

Danish Energy Agency (2022). Energy Statistics 2021.

Danish Ministry of Climate, Energy and Utilities. en.kefm.dk

The Danish Ministry of Taxation (2021). *Stor stigning i antal biler på vejene*.

Egan Sjölander, A. et al. (2014). *Motorspriten kommer!: en historia om etanol och andra alternativa drivmedel*. Gidlunds förlag.

Ekerholm, H. (2012). *Bränsle för den moderna nationen: Etanol och gengas i Sverige under mellankrigstiden och andra världskriget*. Umeå Universitet.

Energy Facts Norway. energifakta.no.

Engen, S. et al. (2023). Small hydropower, large obstacle? Exploring land use conflict, Indigenous opposition and acceptance in the Norwegian Arctic. *Energy Research & Social Science, 95*, 102888, ISSN 2214-6296. https://doi.org/10.1016/j.erss.2022.102888

Equinor. equinor.com

EURACTIV.com (2021). Renewables cover over half of Finland's electricity production.

Fellman, S. (2008). Growth and Investment: Finnish Capitalism, 1850–2005. In S. Fellman et al., *Creating Nordic Capitalism: The Business History of a Competitive Periphery*. Palgrave-Macmillan.

Fellman, S. et al. (2008). *Creating Nordic Capitalism: The Business History of a Competitive Periphery*. Palgrave-Macmillan.

Fridlund, M. (1999). Procuring Products and Power: Developing International Competitiveness in Swedish Electrotechnology and Electric Power. In C. Edquist (Eds.), *Public Technology Procurement and Innovation*, Economics of Science, Technology and Innovation 16. Kluwer Academic Publishers.

Grimstedt, O. (1995). Mutual Trust. The purchasing of the first Swedish commercial reactor. In A. Kaijser & M. Hedin (Eds.), *Nordic Energy Systems. Historical Perspectives and Current Issues*. Science history Publication.

Fortum.com. fortum.com/energy-production

Haikola, S. & Anshelm, J. (2016). Power production and environmental opinions: Environmentally motivated resistance to wind power in Sweden. *Renewable & sustainable energy reviews, 57*, 1545–1555. https://doi.org/10.1016/j.rser.2015.12.211

Hanisch, T. J. & Nerheim G. (1992). *Norsk oljehistorie. Fra vantro til overmot?* Leseselskapet.

Hansen, E. & Jespersen, L. (2009). *Samfundsplanlægning i 1950'erne – Tradition eller tilløb?* Museum Tusculanums Forlag.

Hyldtoft, O. (1995). *Den lysende gas. Etableringen af det danske gassystem 1800–1890*. Systime.

Högselius, P. & Kaijser, A. (2007). *När folkhemselen blev internationell: Elavregleringen i historiskt perspektiv*. Stockholm, SNS Förlag.

Högselius, P. (2009). The internationalization of the European electricity industry: The case of Vattenfall. *Utilities Policy, 17*(3), 258–266.

Högselius, P. et al. (2016). *Europe's Infrastructure Transition. Economy, War, Nature.* Palgrave Macmillan.

International Energy Agency. IEA data over net energy imports up until 2020 (Europe – Countries & Regions – IEA).

International Hydropower Association. hydropower.org/iha/discover-history-of-hydropower

Jacobsson, E. (1996). *Industrialisering av älvar. Studier kring svensk vattenkraftutbyggnad 1900–1918.* Historiska Institutionen, Göteborg.

Jensen-Eriksen, N. (2020). Looking for cheap and abundant power: Business, government and nuclear energy in Finland. *Business History*, vol. 64 No. 8, 1413-1434. https://doi.org/10.1080/00076791.2020.1772761

Jensen-Eriksen, N. (2007) The first wave of the Soviet oil offensive: The Anglo–American Alliance and the flow of 'Red Oil' to Finland during the 1950s. *Business History*, (49)3, 348–366. https://doi.org/10.1080/00076790701295011

Jåfs, D. (2009). *Introduktionen av kärnkraften i Finland: en undersökning med fokus speciellt på vår verkstadsindustris roll.* Åbo Akademis förlag.

Kaijser, A. (1986). Stadens ljus: etableringen av de första svenska gasverken. Dissertation, Linköping University.

Kaijser, A. & Högselius, P. (2019). Under the Damocles Sword. Managing Swedish energy dependence in the twentieth century. *Energy Policy, 126,* 157–164.

Kaijser, A. & Meyer, J. (2018) "The World's Worst Located Nuclear Power Plant": Danish and Swedish Cross-Border Perspectives on the Barsebäck Nuclear Power Plant. *Journal for the History of Environment and Society, 3.* https://doi.org/10.1484/J.JHES.5.116795

Kander, A. (2002). *Economic growth, energy consumption and CO2 emissions in Sweden 1800–2000*. Almqvist & Wiksell International.

Lagendijk, V. & van der Vleuten, E. (2013), Inventing Electrical Europe: Interdependencies, Borders, Vulnerabilities. In A. Hommels et al., *The Making of Europe's Critical Infrastructures*. Palgrave MacMillan.

Lange, E. (2015). *Industrisamfunnets vekst og velstandsøkning*. https://www.norgeshistorie.no/velferdsstat-og-vestvending/1807-industrisamfunnets-vekst-og-velstandsøkning.html

Lerøen, B. V. (2019). *Statoil as a red thread in Norway's oil model*. https://statfjord.industriminne.no/en/2019/11/11/statoil-as-a-red-thread-in-norways-oil-model/

Lundberg, C. (2009). *Vattenfall. Ett bolag i statens tjänst*. Uppsala Universitet. Ekonomisk historia.

Lundin, P. (2008). *Bilsamhället: Ideologi, expertis och regelskapande i efterkrigstidens Sverige*. Stockholmia Förlag.

Johansson, Bengt O. H. (1997). *Den stora stadsomvandlingen: erfarenheter från ett kulturmord*. Arbetsgruppen för arkitektur och formgivning, Regeringskansliet.

Majava, A. et al. (2022) Sectoral low-carbon roadmaps and the role of forest biomass in Finland's carbon neutrality 2035 target. *Energy Strategy Reviews*, 41. https://doi.org/10.1016/j.esr.2022.100836

Matala, S. (2022) National Security, Security of Supply. Finlandisation as a Diplomatic Practice and the Finnish Energy Dependency on the Soviet Union, 1948–1992. *The International History Review* Vol. 45 No. 3, 551-571. https://doi.org/10.1080/07075332.2022.2155212

Maudsley, A. (2022). *Swedish planning and development in the 20th and 21st centuries*. Taylor and Francis.

Meinander, H. (2020). *Finlands historia*. Lind & Co.

Melsted, O. (2020). *Icelandic Energy Regimes Fossil Fuels, Renewables, and the Making of a Low-carbon Energy Balance, 1940-1980*. Dissertation, University of Innsbruck.

Michelsen, K.-E. (2013). An Uneasy Alliance: Negotiating Infrastructures at the Finnish-Soviet Border. In A. Hommels et al., *The Making of Europe's Critical Infrastructures*. Palgrave-MacMillan.

Millkrantz, J. et al. (2022). Petrokultur och energihistoria. *Scandia, 88*(1), 127-140.

Mitchell, T. (2013). *Carbon Democracy: Political Power in the Age of Oil*. Verso Books.

Mustonen, T. et al. (2010). *Drowning Reindeer, Drowning Homes: Indigenous SÁMI and Hydroelectricity Development in Sompio, Finland*. Snowchange Cooperative.

Myllyntaus, T. (1991). *Electrifying Finland. The transfer of a new technology into a late industrialising economy*. The Research Institute of the Finnish Economy.

Myllyntaus, T. (2011). Farewell to Self-sufficiency: Finland and the Globalization of Fossil Fuels. In M. Järvelä & S. Juholam (Eds.), *Energy, Policy, and the Environment: Modeling Sustainable Development for the North*. Springer.

National Energy Authority, NEA, Iceland. www.orkustofnun.is

Nielsen, H. et al. (1998). *Til samfundets tarv – Forskningscenter Risøs historie*. Forskningscenter Risø.

Nordics.info. nordics.info

Norwegian Petroleum Directorate, NPD. norwegianpetroleum.no

Nukissiorfiit. nukissiorfiit.gl/da/

NunaGreen Ltd. nunagreen.gl

Nye, D. E. (2001). *Consuming Power. A Social History of American Energies*. MIT Press.

Our World in Data. ourworldindata.org

Painter, D. S. (2009). The Marshall Plan and oil. *Cold War History, 9*(2), 159-175. https://doi.org/10.1080/14682740902871851

Petersen, F. (1996). *Atomalder uden kernekraft. Forsøget på at indføre atomkraft i Danmark 1954-1985 set i internationalt perspektiv.* Klim.

Petersen, F. (2017). *Da Danmark fik vinger. Vindmøllehistorien 1978-2018.* Danmarks Vindmølleforening.

Pfister, C. (2010). The "1950s syndrome" and the transition from a slow-going to a rapid loss of global sustainability. In F. Uekötter (Ed.), *Turning Points in Environmental History* (2020). University of Pittsburgh Press.

Pharo, H. Ø. (2015). *Marshallplanen – fra skepsis til omfavnelse.* Norgeshistorie.no

Pomeranz, K. (2000). *The Great Divergence. China, Europe, and the Making of the Modern World Economy.* Princeton.

Ranta, T. et al. (2020). Development of the Bioenergy as a Part of Renewable Energy in the Nordic Countries: A Comparative Analysis. *Journal of Sustainable Bioenergy Systems*, *10*(3), September. https://doi.org/10.4236/jsbs.2020.103008

Rasmussen, S. H. (1997). *Sære alliancer. Politiske bevægelser i efterkrigstidens Danmark.* Odense University.

Ryggvik, A. (2015). Short History of the Norwegian Oil Industry: From Protected National Champions to Internationally Competitive Multinationals. *Business History Review*, 89, Spring, 3-41.

Rüdiger, M. (2011). *Moving energy forward.* DONG Energy.

Rüdiger, M. (2019). *Oliekrisen.* Aarhus Universitetsforlag.

Rüdiger, M. (2021). The breakthrough of the 21 degrees culture in Denmark. Undoing and doing gender in Danish home making after 1945. *Journal of Energy History/Revue* https://Energyhistory.eu/en/node/270

Rüdiger, M. (2022). Tiltrækning og bæredygtighed. *TEMP – Tidsskrift for historie*, 24, 12-29.

Salonen, S. (2021). Sámi representatives in COP26 raise concerns over 'green colonialism.' *The Independent Barent Observer.*

SEV. sev.fo

Sjödin, J. (2003). Swedish district heating systems and a harmonised European energy market: means to reduce global carbon emissions. Dissertation, Linköping University.

Sjögren, H. (2008). Welfare Capitalism: The Swedish Economy 1850-2005. In S. Fellman et al., *Creating Nordic Capitalism: The Business History of a Competitive Periphery*. Palgrave Macmillan.

StatBank Greenland. bankstat.gl

Statistics Denmark. dst.dk

Statistics Denmark. (1964). *Tiårsoversigten*.

Statistics Denmark. (2014). *60 år i tal – Danmark siden 2. verdenskrig*.

Statistics Finland statistics database. https://pxdata.stat.fi/PxWeb/pxweb/en/StatFin/

Statistics Norway. ssb.no

Stattnett. (2022). Import and export for the period 2010-2021. https://www.statnett.no/en/for-stakeholders-in-the-power-industry/data-from-the-power-system/import-and-export-for-the-period-2012-2021/

Swedish Energy Agency. (2022). Energiläget 2022. Med energibalanser för år 1970-2020. (ET 2022: 9).

Swedish Energy Agency Statistics database. https://pxexternal.energimyndigheten.se/pxweb/sv/

Sylvest, C. (2022). *Atomfrygt*. Aarhus Universitetsforlag.

Thomsen, H. & Thorndahl, J. (2007). *El og gas til de danske kommuner*. Elmuseet, Gasmuseet.

Thorarinsdottir, R. & Loftsdottir, A. S. (2006). *Energy in Iceland. Historical Perspective, Present Status, Future Outlook*. Orkustofnun.

Thue, L. (1996). *Strøm og styring i norsk kraftliberalisme i historisk perspektiv*. Ad notam.

Tilastokeskus/Statistics Finland. (2022). https://pxdata.stat.fi/PxWeb/pxweb/fi/

Toivanen, T. (2021). A Player Bigger Than Its Size: Finnish Bioeconomy and Forest Policy in the Era of Global Climate Politics. In Backhouse, M. et al., *Bioeconomy and Global Inequalities*. Palgrave Macmillan. https://doi.org/10.1007/978-3-030-68944-5_7

Tolnov Clausen, L. et al. (2021). The good process or the great illusion? A spatial perspective on public participation in Danish municipal wind turbine planning. *Journal of Environmental Policy & Planning, 23*(6), 732–751. https://doi.org/10.1080/1523908X.2021.1910017

TransportochLogistik.se. (2023). *Elbilar dominerar i Norge.*

Vattenfall. vattenfall.com

Vinichenko, V. et al. (2021). Historical precedents and feasibility of rapid coal and gas decline required for the 1.5 C target. *One Earth, 4*, 1477–1490. https://doi.org/10.1016/j.oneear.2021.09.012

Voldsgaard, A. & Rüdiger, M. (2021). Innovative Enterprise, Industrial Ecosystems and Sustainable Transition: The Case of Transforming DONG Energy to Ørsted. In M. Lackner et al. (Eds.), *Handbook of Climate Change Mitigation and Adaptation*. SpringerLink.

Wistoft, B. et al. (1992). *Elektricitetens Aarhundrede. Dansk Elforsynings historie*, Vol. 2. Danske Elværkers Forening.

Worldbank. worldbank.org

York, R. & Bell, S. E. (2019). Energy transitions or additions? Why a transition from fossil fuels requires more than the growth of renewable energy. *Energy Research & Social Science, 51*, 40–43.

Ørsted. orsted.com

Össbo, Å. & Lantto, P. (2011). Colonial Tutelage and Industrial Colonialism: reindeer husbandry and early 20th-century hydroelectric development in Sweden. *Scandinavian Journal of History, 36*(3), 324–348. https://doi.org/10.1080/03468755.2011.580077

Össbo, Å. (2018) Recurring Colonial Ignorance: A Genealogy of the Swedish Energy System. *Journal of Northern Studies*, 12(2), 63–80.

Össbo, Å. (2023). Hydropower histories and narrative injustice: state-owned energy companies' narratives of hydropower expansion in Sápmi. *Water History*. https://doi.org/10.1007/s12685-023-00328-z

Österlin, C. & Raitio, K. (2020). Fragmented Landscapes and Planscapes – The Double Pressure of Increasing Natural Resource Exploitation on Indigenous Sámi Lands in Northern Sweden. *Resources, 9*, 104. https://doi.org/10.3390/resources9090104

Åberg, A. (2013). *A Gap in the Grid. Attempts to Introduce Natural Gas in Sweden 1967–1991*. Royal Institute of Technology.

Åberg, A. & Fjaestad, M. (2020). Chasing Uranium: Securing nuclear fuel on a transnational arena in Sweden 1971–1984. In special issue "Creating, Capturing and Circulating Commodities: Technology and politics of resource flows 19th century to the present day", *Extractive Industries and Society, 7*(1), 2020, 29–38. https://doi.org/10.1016/j.exis.2019.07.003